DIGITAL TWIN FRAMEWORK

A PRACTICAL GUIDE

MAY 2025

ASIAN DEVELOPMENT BANK

6 ADB Avenue, Mandaluyong City, 1550 Metro Manila, Philippines
Tel +63 2 8632 4444; Fax +63 2 8636 2444
www.adb.org

ISBN 978-92-9277-296-3 (print); 978-92-9277-297-0 (PDF); 978-92-9277-298-7 (ebook)
Publication Stock No. SPR250158
DOI: http://dx.doi.org/10.22617/SPR250158

Corrigenda to ADB publications may be found at http://www.adb.org/publications/corrigenda.

Note:
In this publication, "$" refers to United States dollars, unless otherwise specified.
ADB recognizes "China" as the People's Republic of China.

Cover design by Jan Carlo dela Cruz (photo by ADB).

CONTENTS

TABLES, FIGURES, AND BOXES

Tables

Figures

Boxes

FOREWORD

We are pleased to share with you the *Digital Twin Framework* of the Asian Development Bank (ADB), which is intended to enable ADB and its developing member countries (DMCs) to leverage this innovative technology for enhancing infrastructure design and operations.

As the name indicates, digital twins are high-fidelity representations of real-world physical assets or infrastructure. They are connected to their real-world counterparts to reflect their performance and condition. The virtual models are developed based on aggregated real-time or near-real-time data; created using software; and are being used for analyses, simulations, and predictions. The versatility of digital twins has allowed various industries to utilize the technology to transform their operations—including enjoying lower operation, maintenance, and replacement costs; and creating infrastructure designs that are optimized for future threats, such as climate change. By providing accurate and real-time data to decision-makers, digital twins can improve a government's service delivery and support decision-making, which will ultimately benefit communities.

Digital twins are complex as they often involve data harmonization from multiple stakeholders. They also require capital costs to set up and sustain their operations. ADB is ready to provide technical and financial assistance to DMCs so they could leverage this innovative technology not only to enhance infrastructure design and operations but also to help sustainably address the region's infrastructure deficit. It is noted that developing Asia alone needs to invest $1.7 trillion per year in infrastructure to maintain its growth momentum, eradicate poverty, and respond to climate change. Digital twins can provide critical support to make public infrastructure planning, design, and construction faster, cheaper, and more durable against risks.

Mainstreaming digital twins can be considered as an investment for the future. Not only can this technology help increase infrastructure's resilience to climate impacts, but it can also be used for future-proofing urban environments. While digital twins are currently considered "nice to have" in infrastructure projects, we foresee that these will later be seen as "must-have" inclusions in the public infrastructure sphere due to their many benefits.

We are at the planning stages of a "Digital Twin Studio," which will serve as a collaborative area where stakeholders and governments, including experts in technology and engineering that are keen on climate-proofing initiatives, can come together and identify ways in which the technology can be leveraged in specific contexts. This will contribute to ADB's vision of achieving a prosperous, inclusive, resilient, and sustainable Asia and the Pacific.

Stephanie KC Hung
Director General
Information Technology Department
Asian Development Bank

MESSAGE

As the world becomes increasingly interconnected and technology evolves at a more rapid pace, the need for emerging markets and developing member countries (DMCs) to harness transformative and innovative technologies has never been more pressing. As DMCs strive for inclusive economic growth, sustainable development, and improved resilience, they face a dual challenge of addressing historical infrastructure gaps and keeping pace with the demands of digital modernization. One of the most transformative technologies today is digital twins. These virtual models of physical objects, systems, and/or processes enable real-time monitoring, simulation, and optimization, thus offering previously unprecedented opportunities to manage systems that are in critical need of modernization such as infrastructure, energy, agriculture, and health care, among many others.

For DMCs, the adoption of digital twin technologies can be a game changer. Digital twins can be used not just for modeling complex systems, but also to drive innovation and efficiency gains in resource management, infrastructure planning, and informed decision-making.

At the Asian Development Bank, we are already testing how digital twins can improve programs in Asia and the Pacific. For example, in Uzbekistan, digital twins were used for smart road construction that is more environment-friendly and sustainable, offers value for money, and best fits local contexts. The digital platform allows users to compare simulations of road designs and available local materials to identify which pavement solutions are the most sustainable, resilient, and cost-effective. In urban design, digital twins are being used for visualization, analysis, and evaluation of the performance of urban and dispersed physical infrastructure by combining data from multiple sources, such as land monitoring systems, aerial surveys, satellite data, mobile location systems, census data, and Open Data. In Indonesia, a regional geodigital twin model is being used to inform improved investments, disaster risk reduction, forest sequestration, the modeling of transport emissions, and policymaking.

Digital twins allow governments and businesses to make better data-informed decisions, reduce risks, and allocate resources more effectively. As the technology landscape morphs and accelerates, so too must the DMCs' ability to predict, pivot, prepare, and adapt. Digital twins provide one pathway to creating smarter cities, more efficient resource management, greater collaboration with the private sector, and ultimately improved economic resilience and growth.

F. Cleo Kawawaki
Director General
Sectors Department 2
Asian Development Bank

ACKNOWLEDGMENTS

The *Digital Twin Framework* was developed through the Digital Innovation Sandbox Program of the Asian Development Bank's Information Technology Department (ITD).

The team would like to thank all those who provided their time and expertise in developing the framework. ITD and the Climate Change and Sustainable Development Department provided guidance, which was led by Ozzeir Khan (former director of the Digital Innovation and Architecture Division), Thomas Abell (former director of the Digital Technology for Development Division), Marc Lepage (principal IT specialist), and Ritchie Anne Guzman Roño (consultant). Colleagues who also provided valuable contributions in the preparation of this framework include Byeongjo Kong (digital technology specialist); Elizabeth Jung (urban development specialist); Geoffrey Wilson (senior water resources specialist); Hong Soo Lee (senior urban development specialist); Alexander Nash (senior urban development specialist); Jinqiang Chen (urban development specialist); Mikio Mukai (principal IT specialist); Nargiza Talipova (advisor and head of the Project Management Unit of the Strategy, Policy, and Partnerships Department); Okju Jeong (climate change specialist); Paolo Manunta (senior digital technology specialist); Pawan Karki (principal transport specialist); Len George (principal energy specialist); Pivithuru Indrawansa (senior project officer); Ron Durante (Data Services Team); and Satoshi Ishii (director of Strategy and Partnerships).

Thanks are also extended to the working team of AWR Lloyd and Aurecon.

Special thanks go to those who undertook the technical editing and design of this document for their invaluable support in preparing it for publication.

ABBREVIATIONS

ADB	Asian Development Bank
AI	artificial intelligence
BIM	building information modeling
CAD	computer-aided design
CAPEX	capital expenditure
DFI	development finance institution
DMC	developing member country
DMF	Design and Monitoring Framework
Gen AI	generative AI
GIS	geographic information system
IoT	Internet of Things
NASA	National Aeronautics and Space Administration
O&M	operations and maintenance
OP	operational priority
OPEX	operational expenditure
OT	operational technology
ROI	return on investment
SDOs	standards development organizations
SPADE	Spatial Data Analysis Explorer
TOR	terms of reference

EXECUTIVE SUMMARY

Climate extremes and related disasters lead to complexities in infrastructure development. Extreme weather events increase risks, prolong construction, and escalate financing expenses, ultimately lowering asset utilization and disrupting revenue plans. Climate-resilient infrastructure will not only help reduce direct losses and indirect costs of disruption, but it is also central to the region's social and economic prosperity and Sustainable Development Goals. Asia and the Pacific requires significant investments to become more resilient against complex challenges. A study of infrastructure investment needs across 45 developing economies in Asia and the Pacific estimated the total required from 2016 to 2030 as at least $1.5 trillion per year, rising to $1.7 trillion annually when including climate mitigation and adaptation costs (ADB 2017).

Technology can be used in infrastructure development to aid sustainability and climate resilience. Within the climate context, quality infrastructure investments will remain a key priority for ADB, critically driven by technology to enable green, inclusive, and resilient infrastructure. Emerging and disruptive digital technologies have the potential to enhance critical infrastructure resilience by providing a rapid and accurate assessment of asset conditions to support decision-making and adaptation.

Digital twins offer a solution that connects the physical and digital worlds to improve the resiliency and sustainability of the infrastructure asset across its life cycle. Digital twins can be tailored to provide a multitude of cross-sector applications and benefits. These include (i) reduced infrastructure operating and maintenance costs; (ii) diminished risks from natural hazard events (e.g., flooding) and system failure; and (iii) optimized infrastructure design, engineering, and construction. It is estimated that the market for digital twins will continue to grow at a compound annual rate of 36% until 2025 and, based on Dassault Systèmes and Accenture (2021), it could unlock a combined additional benefit of $1.3 trillion in economic value and an emissions reduction of 7.5 gigatons of carbon dioxide equivalent by 2030.

This *Digital Twin Framework* offers a way for users to learn how to harness digital twins in the development of resilient and sustainable infrastructure. It serves as a guidance document and tool kit for stakeholders—to primarily help them develop a foundational understanding of digital twins toward making informed procurement and investment decisions. It also offers tools and guidance that could facilitate the design and building of digital twins to meet their specific use-cases, in accordance with globally recognized values, principles, and industry best practices.

1 INTRODUCTION TO DIGITAL TWINS

1.1 What is a Digital Twin?

The concept of "digital twins" emerged from the National Aeronautics and Space Administration (NASA) in the 1960s when it developed a digital twin to assess and simulate conditions for its Apollo 13 moon mission. However, the term "digital twin" was first publicly introduced by Grieves in 2002 (Grieves and Vickers 2017) where it was defined in the context of product life-cycle management as "a set of virtual information constructs that fully describes a potential or actual physical manufactured product from the micro atomic level to the macro geometrical level." The very technical and context-specific definition of a digital twin has since become more generalized through industry use and cross-adoptions over the years.

Some recent definitions of digital twins from multinational companies, government authorities, academia, consulting firms, and nonprofit organizations, include the following:

> ***"... a virtual representation of an object or system that spans its lifecycle, is updated from real-time data, and uses simulation, machine learning and reasoning to help decision making."***
>
> —M. M. Armstrong (n.d.), IBM

> ***"... a living model that drives a business outcome. The model constantly accumulates operational and environmental data to continuously update itself."***
>
> —Minds + Machines: Meet a Digital Twin (a video)

> ***"A living digital representation of an individual physical system that is dynamically updated with data to mimic the true structure, state, and behavior of the physical system, to drive business outcomes."***
>
> —A. Rasheed (2022), Amazon Web Services

> ***"... digital representation of assets, processes, or systems in the built or natural environment."***
>
> —D. Philp (2021)

> ***"A virtual representation of real-world entities and processes, synchronized at a specified frequency and fidelity."***
>
> —Olcott and Mullen (2020)

> ***"... cyber-physical computational systems that pair the virtual and physical worlds using iterative feedback loops between measurable data acquired from the physical world and simulated processes and behaviors acquired from the virtual world."***
>
> —Smart City Digital Twin Convergence Workshop: FINAL REPORT (2019), Georgia Institute of Technology

> ***"A digital replica that imparts some form of intelligence and agency into the entities being twinned to achieve the desired function."***
>
> —Agrawal, Singh, and Fischer (2022)

> ***"... a digital representation of a real-world entity or system."***
>
> —Gartner (n.d.)

As evident in these definitions, there is no consensus on a universally accepted definition of a digital twin. A single, commonly accepted definition of digital twin is not found in literature due to several factors that make each digital twin unique—such as the nature and scale of the real-world "subject" it seeks to mirror, or *twin*. For instance, the subject of a digital twin could be a bridge, the traffic system connected to the bridge, an entire satellite city, or it may even be feasible for an entire ecosystem of digital twins to represent metropolitan cities or even a nation in its entirety. Similar to the subject, there are various factors, such as the classification, maturity levels, enabling technologies, fidelity, and frequency that need to be synchronized at varying degrees to serve the particular application or use-case of a digital twin.

Combining the fundamental commonalities in the context of this framework for the Asian Development Bank (ADB), a digital twin can be defined as:

> ***"A virtual twin of an infrastructure asset, that gathers data from the built environment at a specific frequency (typically real-time or near-real-time data streams) and visualizes computational models at a specific fidelity."***

Digital twins can vary in complexity and sophistication depending on the specific outcome(s) they are trying to achieve. These outcomes could include improving design, monitoring and verifying as-built situation, running "what-if" simulations and conducting scenario analysis, and so forth. **Due to such complexity, it is highly recommended that one begins with a** Digital Twin Lite (refer to Section 2 for details).

1.2 Foundations of a Digital Twin

Despite the lack of a universally accepted definition of a digital twin, there are, however, several commonalities among most definitions that set the "foundations" for what a digital twin should be. A technological solution can be classified as a digital twin if it is built on all of the following foundations:

Foundation #1: A digital twin must involve the flow of data from the physical world.

A digital twin is built on data collected through various means but must include real-time or near-real-time data from sensors and observations to realize the physical world. These data sources (e.g., sensors) can measure various parameters, such as greenhouse gas emissions, natural resource (e.g., air, water, soil) quality, temperature, wind speed, and others, and provide data updates at a specific time or "frequency" as required by the use-case of the digital twin. The frequency of synchronization of a digital twin may vary (i.e., real time, daily, in batches, milestones, and others), depending on how rapidly the real-world entities will change (e.g., from a fraction of a second to days) and the synchronization mechanisms available and suitable to capture the changes of the physical counterpart.

Foundation #2: A digital twin is a dynamic representation of the physical world.

Using dynamic data models, digital twins emulate and recreate the physical world on a virtual platform. Depending on the purpose, it may incorporate the geometry, attributes, and behaviors, or represent an entire life cycle of a system—from design and manufacturing to operation and maintenance (O&M). The level of accuracy, reliability, and completeness or **"fidelity"** of the data will depend on the intended function of the digital twin. The fidelity of a digital twin characterizes the degree of precision and accuracy applied to the virtual representation and only needs to be sufficient for the desired use-case(s).

Foundation #3: A digital twin is built to serve a purpose.

For each and every digital twin, the use-case and intended outcome(s) are unique. For instance, one could use a digital twin as a tool to measure an infrastructure asset's performance, while another could use a digital twin to remotely monitor the construction or operations of the infrastructure. This capability depends on the purpose as well as the complexity of the digital twin implementation, which is contingent to the combination of enabling technologies being used (Foundation #5).

Foundation #4: A digital twin requires updates to remain effective.

The physical world evolves over time, and therefore, an effective digital twin will evolve along with it in order to remain accurate and relevant. Updating the digital twin to reflect changes in the physical system, technological advancements, and advances in understanding are critical to maintaining its effectiveness.

Foundation #5: A digital twin unlocks further insights as it matures.

The complexity and sophistication of digital twins are referred to as "maturity levels" that enable users to select the scale of digital twin implementation that is appropriate to their domains of practice. These technologies are essential building blocks for creating a purpose-built digital twin. The more mature they become, the higher their potential to unravel insights.

As digital twins mature through progressively incorporating layers of technology, they have the capacity to assimilate increasing amounts of data and analyze them in a multitude of ways. With this, digital twins can perform increasingly "intelligent" tasks with human aid, or even autonomously.

Coupled with the ever-growing advancements in technology, compounding the synergistic capabilities of multiple-connected digital twins to derive richer insights and value will often surpass human foresight and cognition (Figure 1).

Digital twins can be further understood in terms of what they are ***not***. Section 1.3 covers some key misconceptions about digital twins.

So far, digital twins have shown remarkable versatility and have permeated a multitude of industries, transforming the way operations are conducted. From optimizing manufacturing processes to revolutionizing health care delivery, the applications are vast and varied, and the same is true in an infrastructure setting. In the face of extreme climate conditions and its impact on asset development and maintenance, the creation of resilient and sustainable infrastructure that are able to both mitigate climate risks and contribute to their reduction has become increasingly important. Digital twins can potentially conduct "what-if" scenarios, enable predictive maintenance, understand flood risk, and optimize energy usage or public transport. Through their versatility and continually expanding uses, they can play a crucial role in urban planning and infrastructure development, enabling cities to become smarter and more sustainable. The value of this technology is only expected to increase with time, especially given its ability to magnify safety and resilience (Grieves 2023).

Figure 1: Scaling Up Individual Units of a Digital Twin

Source: Author.

1.3 Key Misconceptions

The extensive range of digital twin use-cases for various sectors and user domains perpetuated various industry-specific definitions. Thus, it is common to misconstrue what does and what does not constitute a digital twin. To demystify this concept, it is crucial to identify these common misconceptions and ultimately avoid limiting a digital twin's scope of applicability to just a single definition (refer to Appendix 1 for other misconceptions and challenges regarding digital twins).

Digital twin is a stand-alone technology.

A digital twin is a combination of different enabling technologies (Section 1.4) that assimilates data and combines them to generate insights into business outcomes. Depending on these combinations, the function of a digital twin can vary significantly—ranging from simulation, prediction, to autonomous decision-making.

Building information modeling (BIM) is the same as a digital twin.

Although the two are in essence a digital representation of the physical subject, BIM is typically a static representation that uses preexisting data sources in the modeling process. Due to this ability, BIM's strengths are in closing silos and optimizing the design and construction phase with what exists and is needed, often for a well-defined single asset.

Digital twins, on the other hand, adds breadth and depth to the visualization as they involve automatic or near-automatic data exchanges from the physical subject to its virtual twin. In other words, they allow the physical subject to be truly represented in the context of the built environment, as it interacts with the elements, nature, and people. Due to this ability to integrate environmental and external data, digital twins can have more fluid and rich applications that go beyond design and construction to other aspects, such as operations (Section 2.3 for more details).

Digital twins cannot be built before the physical asset.

A digital twin can be created at any stage of the project or asset life cycle, including the feasibility and design stage before its real-life counterpart is built. Testing different design parameters and studying the implications (e.g., climate impact) prior to the real-life asset being built can offer empirical-based countermeasures to optimize the design. In a road project, for instance, design can be optimized to consider factors such as carbon emissions.

1.4 Key Enabling Technologies

Digital twins are enabled by a combination of technologies to make up the virtual representation of the physical asset, system, or process. Also, the technological configuration of a digital twin varies by its use-case, and depending on its configuration, will yield different value-added benefits that tailor to the requirements of the user. It is worth noting that many of these enabling technologies have been in existence for several decades and have already demonstrated their uses in the context of infrastructure development.

The key enabling technologies referenced in this framework have been identified from the analysis of digital twin use-cases (Appendix 2) and in collaboration with several technology providers.

Data Modeling and Visualization

Data models, data processing algorithms, and data visualization methods enable the representation of datasets related to the physical object (Zhang et al. 2022). Data modeling often includes **BIM, civil information modeling, and other 3D modeling entities,** which utilize a wide variety of modeling languages, such as Unified Modeling Language, and methods to handle data and information modeling. On the other hand, visualization may include **2D/3D computer-aided design (CAD) software (Box 1), augmented reality, and virtual reality,** as well as charts, graphs, and maps that can be used to present the relations among data models and the physical entity in a more intuitive manner and at a level of fidelity desired by the user.

Box 1: 3D Modeling

Three-dimensional (3D) modeling can be extremely useful for capturing the intricate details and geometry of the physical asset. A well-crafted 3D model ensures that the virtual counterpart closely mirrors the real-world object and achieve the level of fidelity that is useful for conducting in-depth analyses and simulations that accurately reflect the physical asset's behavior and performance.

Also, 3D modeling enables an immersive and rich visualization experience within the digital twin environment. Stakeholders—ranging from engineers to decision-makers—can navigate and explore the virtual replica, gaining insights into the physical asset's structure, function, and potential challenges. This experience improves communication, decision-making, and problem-solving processes.

Source: Author.

Internet of Things

Internet of Things (IoT) are physical objects or "things" (e.g., infrastructure component) with embedded computing devices (e.g., sensors) that are interconnected to internet infrastructure through various communication protocols such as Wi-Fi, Bluetooth, and cellular networks (ADB 2021).

They are "smart" as they are embedded with **sensors** that collect data, often in **real time or near real time**, depending on the desired frequency of synchronization of the twin with its physical counterpart. These smart systems gather data pertaining to the physical thing or its surrounding environment[1] and comprise **actuators** that execute predetermined operations in response to this gathered data. The collected data, which are crucial for deriving meaningful insights, are recorded in databases and may undergo processing either locally on the device, at the periphery of the network (i.e., edge computing), and/or in remote servers (i.e., cloud computing).

The principal objective of an IoT is to facilitate communication and information-sharing among these devices in order to enhance decision-making, productivity, and in providing new services. IoT applications often provide a user interface, typically presented through mobile applications or web portals. This interface empowers users to monitor and control interconnected devices, enhancing the overall user experience within the IoT ecosystem.

Spatial Computing

Spatial computing analyzes the geospatial characteristics of the physical entity, using accurate location and dimensional attributes to gain a comprehensive understanding of its spatial environment. Spatial computing processes data acquired from reality capture technologies to visualize the behaviors of a physical entity including its position, orientation, and movement.

Spatial data is increasingly available from a wide variety of sources, including **satellite imagery, geographic information systems (GIS), and remote sensing techniques (Box 2)**. For instance, during the construction of large infrastructure projects, drones or unmanned aerial vehicles—equipped with a camera to capture high-resolution imagery and light detection and ranging or LiDAR lasers—can be used to collect accurate mass point cloud datasets that can be managed using ArcGIS (a specific brand of a suite of GIS software). Visualizing and interacting with physical or digital environments with this spatial context can also be seen through augmented reality and virtual reality applications.

1 These data include human movement, temperature, humidity, lighting, tap sensors, and others.

Box 2: Geographic Information Systems

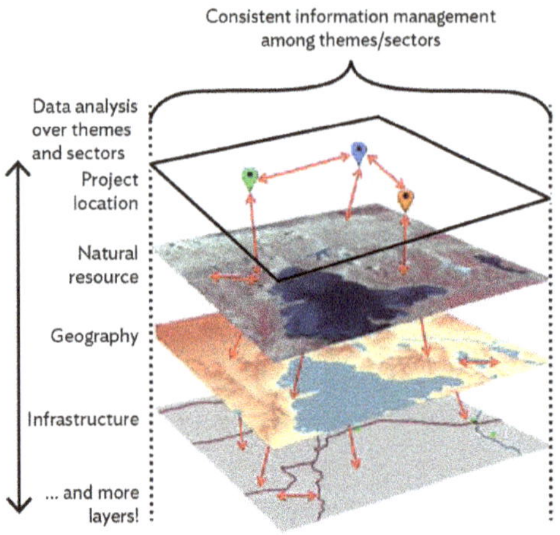

A geographic information system (GIS) is "a system for the management and analysis of geographic information and data." Data sources can include aerial photography data, satellite images, urban planning maps, and thematic maps.

A GIS enables digital twins as it provides a description of the physical environment through a visual display that segments the geographically referenced information into layers.

These layers can be visualized separately such as streets, buildings, vegetation, or in any number of combinations for an isolated view, which unveils hidden connections, such as areas susceptible to natural hazards that can be valuable in disaster prevention. Such applications have found extensive use in Asia.

Source: ADB. 2014. *Space Technology and Geographic Information Systems Applications in ADB Projects.* https://www.adb.org/sites/default/files/publication/148901/space-technology-and-gis-applications-adb-projects.pdf.

Cloud Computing

Cloud computing is the delivery of computing services—including servers, storage, databases, networking, software, analytics, and intelligence—over the internet (the "cloud") to offer faster innovation, flexible resources, and economies of scale (Azure (Microsoft) n. d.).

Cloud computing provides convenient and on-demand access to a shared pool of configurable computing resources that can be rapidly provisioned and released with minimal management effort or service provider interaction. Although only one out of four businesses used cloud computing in 2019, it is estimated that more than 50% of enterprises will use cloud computing by 2028 (Gartner 2023). Also, Asia and the Pacific was the fastest-growing regional cloud market in 2022, experiencing a growth rate of 25% (The Insight Partners 2022).

Since digital twins are built upon unprecedented amounts of datasets, cloud computing plays a key role in the way data are collected, stored, and processed. Cloud computing provides institutions that lack the computing power for big data analysis, with a scalable and flexible infrastructure for implementing digital twins. Other benefits of cloud computing include the following:

- **Cost savings.** Cloud computing eliminates the capital expenses needed to set up an on-site data center, and related operating expenses (e.g., electricity, cooling, IT maintenance, and others).
- **Security.** Cloud computing services operate on a global network of data centers that adhere to a broad set of policies, standards, technologies, and controls that can strengthen system security, enhance data protection, and reduce system vulnerabilities to cyberattacks.
- **Reliability.** Cloud computing offers disaster recovery and business continuity by backing up data at multiple redundant sites.

In many cases, edge computing is used alongside cloud computing. Edge computing is a distributed computing framework that brings enterprise applications closer to data sources, such as IoT devices or local edge servers (IBM n.d.). Edge computing is used to process time-sensitive data and reduce the amount of data that must be computed on the cloud. Besides latency, edge computing is typically preferred over cloud computing in remote locations where there is limited or no connectivity.

Artificial Intelligence

Artificial intelligence (AI) are computer systems that can perform tasks that normally require human intelligence (visual and speech recognition, learning, planning, problem-solving, decision-making, and language translation). AI could arguably have the same level of **economic** and social impact as that of the internet and mobile phones (Harkut and Kasat 2019). AI is also increasingly perceived as a general-purpose technology—a technology that possesses potential to generally transform a wide range of business activities—and so many also argue that it should be widely adopted to develop skills for an AI-enabled economy (Jovanovic and Rousseau 2005; Trajtenberg 2018). Today, AI can have several applications across a number of sectors and can enhance the capabilities of digital twins. For instance, as part of a project in Uzbekistan to upgrade part of the A380 highway, ADB partnered with ORIS, a digital materials platform for sustainable roads, to pilot an AI-enabled digital twin that provides multiple-scenario digital analyses, which generated an alternative design of the highway that optimized its sustainability impact.

AI also broadly **encompasses** several related concepts, such as machine learning, deep learning, and most recently, generative AI (Gen AI) (Figure 2). Although these terms are often used interchangeably, they are not the same (Marr 2016).

Figure 2: Illustration of the Differences Among Artificial Intelligence, Machine Learning, Deep Learning, and Generative Artificial Intelligence

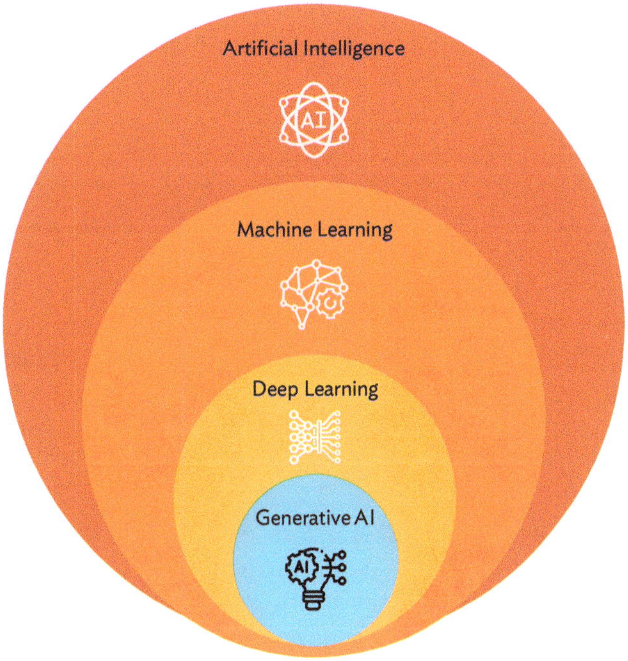

Source: Author.

Machine learning is a subset of AI. AI is the broader concept of machines being able to intelligently carry out tasks, while the concept of machine learning is founded on the principle that machines just require data and can learn by themselves. Hence, machine learning provides systems the ability to automatically learn and improve from experience without being explicitly programmed (Luxton 2016). Deep learning is a subset of machine learning that simulates a human brain, whereby computer systems attempt to learn by examples and perform tasks based on classifying structured and unstructured data. With the growth in computing power, deep learning models are now able to build up ***deep*** neural networks with many layers, such that they can analyze complex nonlinear patterns.

AI, machine learning, and deep learning enable highly complex real-world systems to be accurately modeled as opposed to the more traditional physics-based modeling approaches. As explained by the chief technology officer of General Electric, "When you look at a wind turbine and try to see how to characterize the wind that's coming into that turbine, you quickly realize that wind speed changes based upon the height of the turbine, it is not a constant...It also changes at every hour of the day. That is such a complex thing it can't be modelled by a physical equation... So we use AI and neural nets to model that" (Bui 2023).

One particular branch of AI and a subset of machine learning that has emerged as one of the most promising technological trends for 2023 and beyond is **Gen AI**. According to a 2023 survey by McKinsey, 79% of C-suite executives said they have had at least some exposure to Gen AI tools (McKinsey Global Survey 2023). Gen AI uses machine learning models to learn the patterns and relationships in a dataset of human-created content and then uses the learned patterns to generate new content, including text, audio, images, videos, and even simulations, which have similar characteristics as the reference data (Google Cloud n.d.). Some common examples of Gen AI include image generation using tools like DALL-E 2, Midjourney, and Jasper, but its application can extend to 3D modeling, which is more relevant to digital twins. In fact, some experts—such as Patrick Strauss, chief intelligent environments solutions officer of GlobalLogic (a Hitachi Group Company)—believe that Gen AI is set to revolutionize digital twins by transforming them into "intelligent twins" by the augmentation of the human workforce (Strauss 2023). Not only has the rise of AI been consequently mirrored by the growth of digital twins, AI technology can also support digital twins to perform more complex predictions and enable autonomous learning. The ways in which the power of AI has been instrumental in the proliferation of digital twins can be found in Appendix 3.

1.5 Maturity Levels of Digital Twins

As is the case with most technology adoptions, no digital twin starts off as the most advanced and capable version of itself. Over time, as further complexities and technologies are introduced, it has the potential of becoming a full-fledged or the most "mature" digital twin.

Classifying digital twins based on their level of maturity reflects both the level of data integration with the physical world and the utilization of key enabling technologies. While some opt for a four-level segmentation, most organizations—including technology providers and design and engineering consultants—are using a five-level maturity model (e.g., Centre for Digital Built Britain, Autodesk, Arup, and others) to classify digital twins. This framework follows the latter and adopts the following maturity levels:

- **Level 1—Dynamic Representation.** At this maturity level, the digital twin has the primary feature of aggregating and visualizing data to create a ***dynamic virtual representation*** of its physical counterpart with real- (or near-real) time data from the built environment. Level 1 digital twins are typically used to assess new designs, reconfigurations of brownfield sites, and training personnel.

- **Level 2—Analytics.** At this level, the digital twin incorporates data analytics to generate ***more sophisticated insights and feedback***. As such, Level 2 digital twins can provide performance monitoring, root-cause analysis, dashboard reporting, and statistical metrics.
- **Level 3—Predictive.** At this level, the primary feature is the ability to generate predictions insights through the incorporation of advanced data science or AI capabilities. Level 3 digital twins can inform and predict the personalized behavior and characteristics of their physical counterpart, making them a valuable tool in complex decision-making scenarios.
- **Level 4—Prescriptive.** At this level, the digital twin evolves to incorporate more advanced AI capabilities to generate prescriptive analytics, or in other words, to propose real-time interventions or course of action.
- **Level 5—Cognitive.** This is the highest complexity level of a digital twin as it is capable of ***taking autonomous actions*** and interventions within defined boundaries and can affect real change in the physical twin. A Level 5 digital twin relies on large datasets to recognize patterns and generate precise, corrective actions within the operational environment, minimizing human-to-machine interactions through advanced AI technologies, such as deep learning.

However, much like the definition of digital twins, most stakeholders also have differing perspectives when it comes to the classification or types of digital twins. Diverse classifications exist for digital twins, ranging from classification based on scale of coverage, to ones based on a multidimensional matrix (more information can be found in Appendix 4).

1.6 Digital Twins in the Infrastructure Sector

Below are some examples of digital twin applications in infrastructure projects in Europe, North America, and Asia and the Pacific.

In the **United Kingdom**, a digital twin is being applied during the design-and-build phase of a railway remodeling project, allowing the continued operation of public services at existing railway stations. The digital twin provides a virtual construction platform that allows various stakeholders who may not have a technical or engineering background (designers, public authorities, and others) to efficiently make decisions, among other benefits.

In the **United States**, a digital twin is being applied in the operations and maintenance phase of an aging water distribution system, allowing for seamless integration and visualization of the district-wide network's various components, supported by near-real-time data. Among other benefits, such as reducing water losses or mitigating service disruptions, it allows anomalies to be detected and serves as the foundation for future capabilities, such as crisis simulations.

In **India**, digital twin technology is being applied throughout the entire project life cycle, combining 3D modeling with location data to manage subway assets. This replaces paper records with digital models, ensuring seamless information continuity and accessibility. Among other benefits, such as optimizing workforce requirements and improving cost management, the digital twin is expected to significantly enhance asset reliability and availability, reduce operating costs, and lay the foundation for future capabilities such as predictive maintenance and crisis simulations.

In **Australia**, a digital twin is being applied during the design-and-build phase for a pumped-storage hydropower plant that combines real-time data with 3D modeling and geospatial information. Among other benefits, such as simplifying construction and saving costs, the digital twin enables informed decision-making on the amount of carbon saved during operations.

In **Singapore**, digital twin technology is being applied across the entire life cycle to visualize and plan the urban environment in 3D, integrating topographical and real-time data from various public agencies, thereby ensuring adaptive city development in response to population growth, new construction, and major events. The digital twin helps develop solutions for optimizing logistics, governance, and operations in areas such as environmental management, disaster response, infrastructure, security, and community services—aiding efficient emergency evacuations and enhancing urban living, among other benefits.

In **Malaysia**, a digital twin is being applied throughout the entire life cycle to enhance building information modeling workflows across the Sungai Buloh–Serdang-Putrajaya Line, which is part of Malaysia's mass rapid transit system. This includes visualizing digital assets, checking their real-time status, analyzing data, and optimizing performance. The digital twin enhances decision-making, operational efficiency, and asset management practices, enabling predictive maintenance strategies and laying the foundation for future capabilities such as scenario planning and crisis simulations, among others.

More potential applications of digital twins can be found in the Digital Twin Use-Case Library, which contains more than 200 real-case studies across ADB's main sectors. The library contains descriptions of digital twin projects that can be segmented by sector, asset type, location, or region. It also provides other useful information, such as the technology provider that delivered the project, other quantitative and qualitative benefits from the application, and details on the combination of technologies that enabled the implementation of the digital twin. The range of the various projects illustrates the breadth of digital twins used for different purposes and built at different levels of complexities, as further described in Appendix 5 (Big Data Value 2022).

2 DIGITAL TWIN LITE

2.1 Digital Twins for ADB: Start "Lite"

In the context of the Asian Development Bank (ADB) as a regional development bank and financier of sustainable infrastructure, a **Digital Twin Lite refers to a virtual twin that can be developed during the early stages of the infrastructure or asset life cycle**. This can be done prior to the construction of the underlying physical infrastructure asset(s) or as an improvement or extension to the physical infrastructure asset(s).

Digital Twin Lites are a simplified version of a full-scale digital twin, as their applications are typically limited and are more suitable during the planning and design stages (or prior to the construction of the infrastructure asset). While a Digital Twin Lite retains some of the core functionalities of a traditional digital twin, it is typically limited in terms of its scope and complexity. A Digital Twin Lite is often tailored for specific use-cases rather than providing a comprehensive solution. For example, it may be used for basic monitoring, simple simulations, or preliminary design validation. It is also built upon the premise of proving and realizing value through systematic incrementalism. As suggested by Michael Grieves, executive director and chief scientist for the Digital Twin Institute, the best way to start a digital twin is to "pick the use cases that you're going to do [and] don't try to boil the ocean" (Mangels 2022).

Consequently, it is envisioned that a Digital Twin Lite will serve three key purposes for ADB:

- First, a Digital Twin Lite could be used to aid ADB investment officers during due diligence and investment decision-making processes. For instance, before providing regular, market-based ordinary capital resources loans to developing member countries (DMCs) for the construction of an infrastructure asset, ADB may support DMCs in developing a Digital Twin Lite to stress test the performance of the infrastructure asset under different economic conditions, and to evaluate how resilient the investment is to various market shocks (e.g., pandemics).
- Second, a Digital Twin Lite enables both ADB (lender) and the DMC (borrower) to take corrective actions earlier in the asset's life cycle to improve the construction, and operations and maintenance of this particular infrastructure asset. For instance, historical data and real-time sensor data from the existing built environment surrounding the proposed infrastructure asset can be fed into the Digital Twin Lite to inform the design process. This data-driven design optimization helps in identifying best practices and avoiding past mistakes.
- Third and last, a Digital Twin Lite is envisaged to be scalable after it has been verified and validated (Step 4 of the Road Map for Developing and Scaling a Digital Twin Lite) and handed over to the eventual asset owner(s) of the infrastructure. A Digital Twin Lite not only has the potential to benefit ADB prior to disbursing the loan but also as a means, thereafter, of monitoring and evaluating its investment during the construction, and operations and maintenance of the infrastructure asset throughout the tenor of the loan.

2.2 Why Digital Twin Lite?

Given the hurdles of deploying and realizing the potential value of a full-scale digital twin, starting with a Digital Twin Lite is a strategic approach for DMCs that are looking to harness the benefits of digital twin technology without incurring significant costs, complexity, and time investment associated with full-scale implementations.

It is estimated that digital twins provide an opportunity to seamlessly link and intertwine the physical and digital worlds and have the potential to generate up to $11.1 trillion a year in economic value by 2025 (Bentley n.d.). However, at the same time, full-scale digital twins can be a highly expensive, time-consuming, and expensive undertaking—especially for low-income DMCs that often lack the underlying digital and data infrastructure for a digital twin. For instance, Virtual Singapore, a digital twin of Singapore led by the Singapore Land Authority, is estimated to cost nearly S$73 million (over $50 million) and took more than 5 years to develop.[2]

A Digital Twin Lite has different characteristics compared to a full-scale digital twin (refer to Table 1 for a comparison). It mitigates risks and lays a solid foundation for scaling up to a comprehensive full-scale digital twin in the future, ensuring a smoother transition and more informed investment decisions.

Table 1: Similarities and Differences of a Digital Twin Lite and a Digital Twin

Characteristic	Digital Twin Lite	Digital Twin
Purpose	More flexible, but primarily centers around **demonstrating the proof of value** for a full-scale digital twin	Improves processes across the project's life cycle at scale
Users	Expands to include other primary stakeholders without a technical background, such as shareholders, lenders, and other project team members	Expands to further include multiple stakeholders beyond the project's operational boundaries, such as citizens
Development Time	Weeks to months	Months to years
Complexity	Low to moderate complexity (typically, maturity level 1–3)	Moderate to high complexity (typically, maturity level 2–5)
Investment	Lower cost(typically, <$1 million)	Higher cost (typically, >$5 million)
Use-Case	Specific application and outcomes, due diligence, early feedback, and changes	Wide areas of applications and use-cases at full scale
Others	Suitable for developing member countries (DMCs) at any level of digital readiness; scalable.	Suitable for mature DMCs with a digital agenda and capacity; focus on interoperability.

Source: Author. Adapted from HGA; Varuna; Matterport; Amazon Web Services; Autodesk; Hilcorp; Embassy of Things, Inc.; and the Digital Twin Use-Case Library.

Michael Grieves, executive director and chief scientist for the Digital Twin Institute, coined the term "digital twin" in 2003 with his colleague John Vickers, principal technologist at the National Aeronautics and Space Administration (NASA). He captures the intent of a Digital Twin Lite when he says,

> ***"What I want to do is design the product virtually, test the product virtually, manufacture the product virtually, support the product virtually, and only when I get it all right do I want to move expensive atoms."***
>
> –Michael Grieves (2023)

2 Refer to the use-case library for more information.

2.3 Taking Building Information Modeling to the Next Level with a Digital Twin Lite

Although building information modeling (BIM) or other similar 2D/3D virtual models are often mistaken for a digital twin, the two are not the same but interrelated. **A BIM is a static virtual model of an infrastructure asset during its planning and design stage, while a Digital Twin Lite allows real-time changes from the built environment (such as meteorological data) to be integrated into the model, creating a dynamic model of the infrastructure asset.**

For instance, a BIM in the context of a water infrastructure will have integrated the various components into a single digital model (Celtic Anglian Water 2024). This BIM is data-rich in that each component will now display its unique information, such as the material type, the date of production, the warranty period associated with the piece, and others. The use of BIM allows water engineers, contractors, and operators to collaborate more effectively through the visualization of the BIM models.

On the other hand, the form and layout of a Digital Twin Lite is more flexible—it is not always a detailed digital representation of the infrastructure asset. Although it may be used, a Digital Twin Lite may not require a BIM as its foundation if it is not fit for purpose. Using the same example as above, instead of a 3D model, the Digital Twin Lite may use a data flowchart to more simply convey the water infrastructure and its associated usage. The same component pieces, which can instead be depicted using simple shapes, can contain the same physical information (such as the material type) but through the integration of real- or near-real-time data, it can be extended to include more intelligent analytics such as predicted replacement date for the piece of pipe, and others. As more data become available, the Digital Twin Lite can be expanded into a more robust, data-rich model that supports advanced decision-making and optimization for the water infrastructure, allowing owners and operators to realize the full benefits of this approach (Figure 3).

As a result, a Digital Twin Lite is generally considered as the next progression from a BIM.

Figure 3: Evolution from Building Information Modeling to Digital Twin Lite

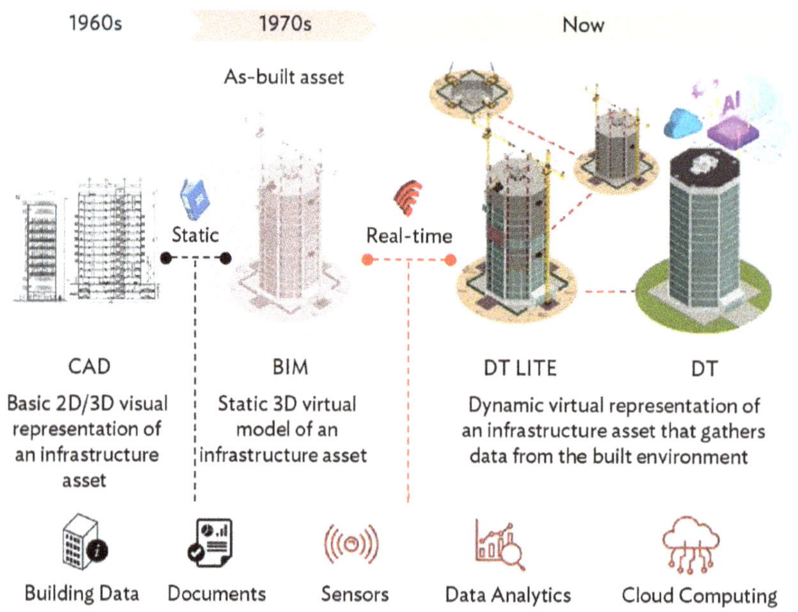

BIM = building information modeling, CAD = computer-aided design, DT = digital twin.
Source: Author.

As compared to BIM, Digital Twin Lites have enhanced capabilities and can be positioned just before the implementation of a full-scale digital twin (Table 2).

Table 2: Similarities and Differences Between a Building Information Modeling and a Digital Twin Lite

Characteristic	Building Information Modeling	Digital Twin Lite
Purpose	Facilitates **ease of coordination during the design and building** of an asset as it allows information to be easily viewed and shared.	More flexible but primarily centers around **demonstrating the proof of value** for a full-scale digital twin
Users	Primarily engineers, architects, and project teams	Expands to include other primary stakeholders without a technical background, such as shareholders and lenders
Key Feature	Presents accurate and comprehensive data in a centralized manner, serving as a single source of truth (SSOT).	In addition to SSOT, it incorporates analytics or other forms of intelligent processing to generate insights or predictions
Enabling Technology	Data modeling and visualization	Different combinations of data modeling and visualization, Internet of Things, spatial computing, cloud computing, and artificial intelligence
Project Life Cycle	Design and build	Planning and design (before construction)
Data Frequency	Static	Near real or real-time
Use-Case	It has limited application primarily in building design and construction.	It has specific application and outcomes, due diligence, early feedback, and changes
Others	It serves as a starting point to build a digital twin	This is suitable for developing member countries at any level of digital readiness and is scalable.

Source: Author. Adapted from Matterport, Amazon Web Services, Autodesk, and others.

2.4 What Makes a Digital Twin Lite Different from a Full-Scale Digital Twin?

The primary distinction of a Digital Twin Lite from a full-scale digital twin is that a Digital Twin Lite is intended for preconstruction infrastructure assets, typically at the planning and/or design phase. As previously discussed, Digital Twin Lites are virtual twins of a to-be or planned infrastructure asset (whether greenfield or an extension to a brownfield asset) with the most common applications being for early-stage visualization, design optimization, collaborative planning, and stakeholder validation. On the other hand, a full-scale digital twin is a more complex and resource-intensive undertaking, which is appropriate for digitally savvy asset owners and developers of large infrastructure projects that are entering or under construction or already operating, with typical applications and focus on enhancing the asset's operational performance, preventive maintenance, and asset management.

In this framework, a Digital Twin Lite is intended to serve as a starting point before building and scaling to a full-scale digital twin. **A Digital Twin Lite is a cost-effective approach to evaluate the technical feasibility and business value proposition of a digital twin under real-world conditions.** A Digital Twin Lite could be a prototype or a pilot that focuses on demonstrating proof of value rather than a traditional proof of concept for the eventual full-scale digital twin, as shown in Figure 4.

Figure 4: Digital Twin Lite As a Proof of Value

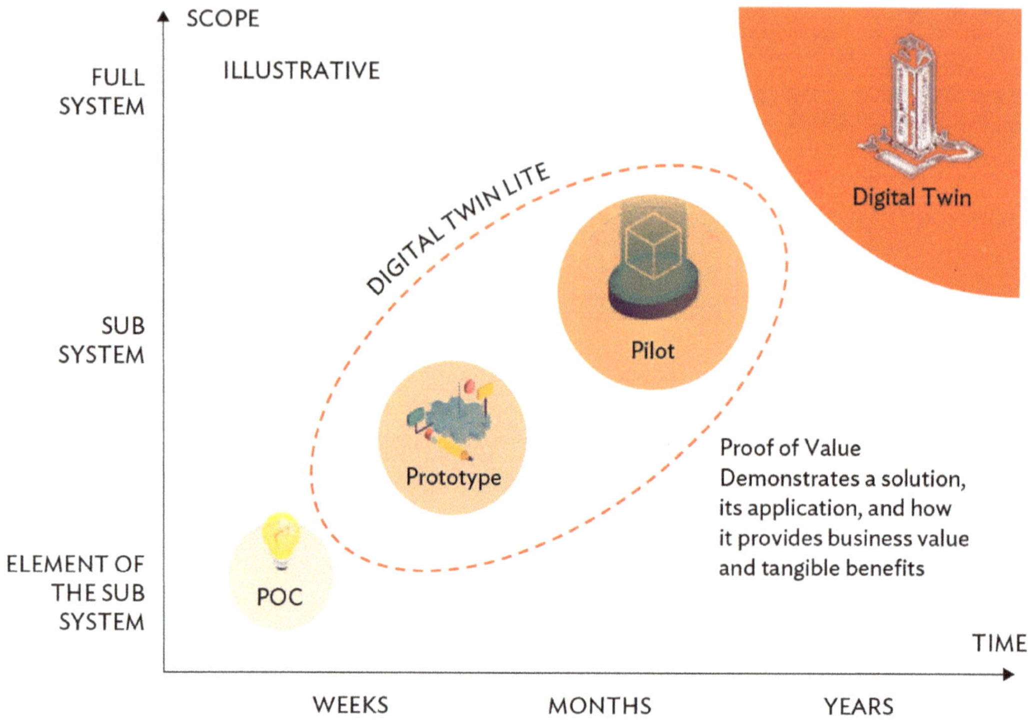

POC = proof of concept.
Source: Author.

By building a Digital Twin Lite first, some early-stage challenges can be resolved, such as upskilling and/or reskilling the relevant government department as necessary and to garner public support. Thus, investment for the eventual full-scale project that will take a couple of months or years to complete as opposed to the weeks and months, **a Digital Twin Lite needs to demonstrate proof of value**. This more manageable and digestible version enables cost- effective risk management on both technical and financial fronts.

Once the technical and business proof of value is established through a Digital Twin Lite, a scaled-up digital twin allows the solution to be accessible and useful for a wider group of stakeholders beyond the project's operational boundaries, such as a citizen's group of a particular district who is now able to consult a water network digital twin to schedule their livelihood around the next predicted and optimized maintenance. Other use-cases beyond the design-and-build phase are possible for a full-scale digital twin, which would be especially suitable for DMCs looking to accelerate their digital agenda and capacity.

2.5 Approach to Digital Twin Lite Development

Most experts **recommend that the Digital Twin Lite should be built progressively following the physical infrastructure asset's life cycle incrementally—from planning, designing, and building, and throughout its operation**. It is envisioned that the Digital Twin Lite will evolve with the asset, thus maintaining an up-to-date record of its history, modifications, and performance metrics. This comprehensive data repository aids in informed decision-making throughout the asset's life cycle.

Typical key use-cases and activities for the Digital Twin Lite as it evolves during each of the infrastructure life-cycle phases are further discussed below.

- **Plan.** During the planning phase of the development of an infrastructure asset, stakeholders typically begin by (i) defining the project's objectives and scope, (ii) conducting research and development, (iii) preparing a feasibility study for the asset, and (iv) assessing the potential impact of the asset (e.g., environmental and social impact assessment).

  During this phase, a Digital Twin Lite can be used as a planning tool (e.g., urban planning tool) or to create preliminary models to simulate various scenarios and stress test the to-be asset under various conditions thereby generating insights into potential challenges and opportunities. During this stage, the typical activities related to the Digital Twin Lite may include conducting geospatial research, mapping and undertaking analysis to form a foundation for a geographic information system (GIS), performing parametric modeling, and administering land management.

- **Design.** During the design phase, detailed plans and specifications of the infrastructure assets are developed. Key activities typically include completing the basic or detailed engineering design, such as the front-end engineering design for the asset.

  During this phase, a Digital Twin Lite is generally used as a tool to aid virtual design collaboration and design optimization and evaluation—by virtually testing the design under different configurations and materials used. It enhances collaboration among technical (e.g., architects and engineers) and nontechnical stakeholders (e.g., planners and policymakers) by providing a shared platform for reviewing and iterating designs and attaining early stakeholder feedback on the to-be design, which lead to optimized and validated solutions before construction begins. During this stage, the usual activities related to the Digital Twin Lite may include data collection through existing technology deployments (e.g., GIS, closed circuit televisions [CCTVs], and others), data migration, data analytics, and preliminary data modeling and BIM.

- **Build.** The build phase involves the physical construction of the infrastructure asset. In this phase, the focus is on procurement and fabrication, resource allocation, construction and assembly, testing and commissioning, and quality assurance.

  During this phase, the typical use-cases of the Digital Twin Lite are for construction management—to provide real-time or near-real-time updates and visualizations of the asset's progress. It can also be used to more intricately monitor and manage resource and material consumption, construction schedules, quality control, and to ensure that the construction of the asset stays on track and within budget. Hence, the typical activities at this stage are often an extension to those at the design phase. For instance, BIM is typically extended into a multidimensional model with additional technology implementations (e.g., Internet of Things [IoT], drone and satellite surveillance, and others) to bolster the data relay and promptly resolve discrepancy (if any) between design and build.

- **Operate and maintain.** During the operation and maintenance (O&M) phase, the completed infrastructure asset is commissioned, tested, put into use, and maintained (and in some cases, enhanced). During this phase, the typical emphases are on asset management, maintenance of operational efficiency, and prevention of failures (or downtime) in the asset.

  During this phase, the Digital Twin Lite continues to provide value by monitoring the asset's performance and condition in real time or near real time by enabling predictive maintenance, optimizing operational efficiency, and reducing downtime. Activities related to the digital twin in this phase include (i) analyzing and securing data related to the asset's maintenance, (ii) ensuring the smooth operations and performance of the asset, and (iii) undertaking a cross-network integration with other infrastructure assets. The virtual twin should continuously evolve with the asset, capturing data on usage patterns and depreciation of the asset, which informs future improvements and issues, thus, ensuring long-term sustainability and resilience.

2.6 At What Stage of the Project's Life Cycle Should a Digital Twin Be Implemented?

While a digital twin can be implemented during any stage of the infrastructure life cycle, most experts generally agree that **implementing a Digital Twin Lite early in the infrastructure life cycle—typically during the planning and design phase—enhances the planning, design, risk management, collaboration, cost efficiency, and scalability that lead to more successful and resilient infrastructure projects.**

While a Digital Twin Lite incurs additional costs and effort during these early stages, as compared with traditional approaches (e.g., computer-aided design [CAD]), its direct (and indirect) benefits—toward the end of the design phase up to the construction and operations phase—often outweigh the cost of implementation. For instance, one study conducted by researchers at the University of Sydney found that globally, 90% of large-scale infrastructure assets incur cost overruns, and that on average, these cost overruns range from 20%–45% of the project costs (Allahaim and Liu n.d.). In this context, Digital Twin Lites, if implemented during the early stages of the infrastructure's life cycle, can theoretically curb (if not eliminate) such cost inflections incurred by infrastructure asset developers and can create cost savings of millions of dollars (refer to Figure 5, which was adapted from MacLeamy Curve (American Architects 2017).

Figure 5: Value Creation of Digital Twins vs. Traditional Computer-Aided Design

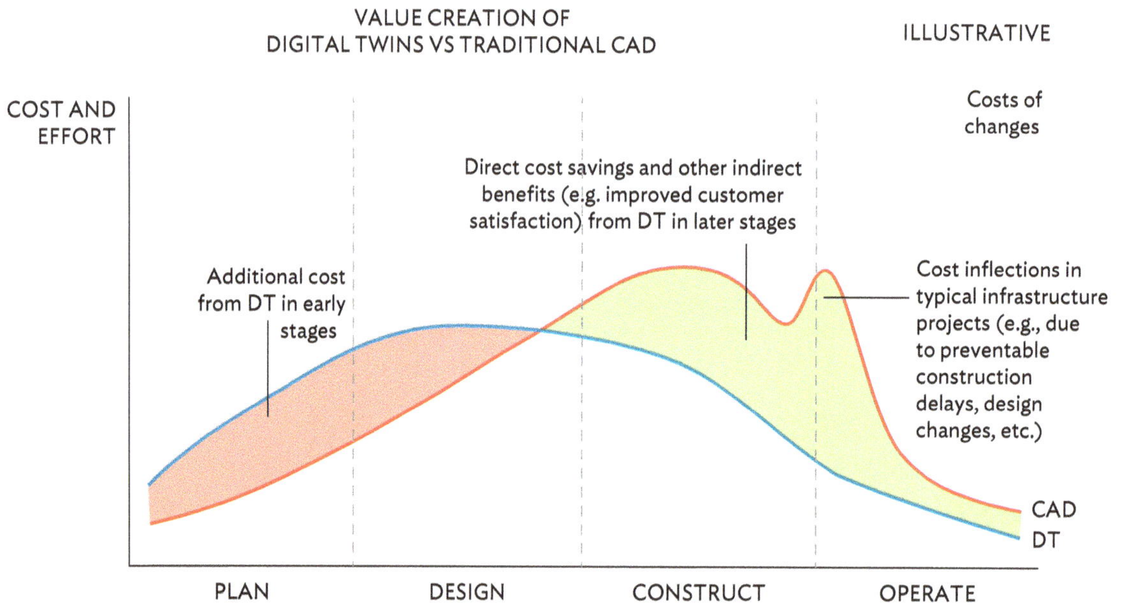

CAD = computer-aided design, DT = digital twin.
Source: Author analysis. Adapted from the MacLeamy Curve (American Architects 2017).

Empirical evidence from reviewing over 200 digital twin case studies globally (Appendix 2 for Use-Case Library) also validates that Digital Twin Lites yield the greatest benefits during the design-and-build stages of infrastructure development. Findings suggest that digital twins implemented during the design-and-build stage, on average, can yield benefits that are around 240% more than that of benefits had the digital twin been implemented during the operate and maintain phase of the infrastructure's life cycle.

2.7 How Can a Digital Twin Lite Be Beneficial to Development Finance Institutions and Developing Member Countries?

Regardless of when a Digital Twin Lite is implemented in an infrastructure asset's life cycle, it can still provide multiple benefits for both the borrower (DMC) and the lender (ADB or any other development finance institution [DFI]) and can facilitate the successful delivery of the planned infrastructure asset by serving as a single source of truth. Some of the ways in which both lenders and borrowers may benefit from a Digital Twin Lite include the following:

- **Contract management.** DFIs generally require DMCs to adhere to stringent contractual covenants for loans or grants. Moreover, financing mechanisms are increasingly linked to nonfinancial measures (e.g., loans linked to environmental, social, and governance). In cases where the financing terms are anchored to specific measures such as performance, outputs and outcomes, budgetary controls, and/or user timelines, a digital twin can serve as a central tool for contract management for both the DFIs and DMCs to monitor their contractual obligations. In addition, Digital Twin Lites can also be used for contract management with third-party affiliates. In some cases, lenders or borrowers themselves may limit the engineering, procurement, and construction contractor's ability to claim additional time and/or resources under the contract. In such cases, digital twins enable data-driven decision-making in assessing these claims.
- **Risk assessment, management, and mitigation.** A Digital Twin Lite allows for a continuous monitoring of the infrastructure asset. This monitoring enables the early detection of anomalies or deviations from normal operations, which are critical for proactive risk management. In this regard, Digital Twin Lites support collaborative risk assessment across DFI and DMC teams and offer benefits such as early risk identification, risk mitigation solutions, and can even prevent failure of critical infrastructure assets.
- **Stakeholder collaboration.** Digital Twin Lites can facilitate collaborative decision-making between DFIs and DMCs. Both parties can interact with Digital Twin Lite to analyze performance trends, simulate what-if scenarios, and discuss potential improvements for the infrastructure asset. This collaborative approach enhances communication and alignment of the goals, financing requirements, and risk mitigation strategies among the parties.

3 ROAD MAP TO DEVELOPING A DIGITAL TWIN

Overview of Digital Twin Road Map and Digital Twin Lite

The Digital Twin Road Map provides a step-by-step guidance for users in developing a digital twin—first, by starting with a Digital Twin Lite (Figure 6).

Figure 6: Overview of the Digital Twin Road Map

	1	2	3	4	5
START	CONCEPTUALIZE	BUSINESS CASE	PROCURE AND BUILD	ASSESS	SCALE
ACTIVITIES	• Conceptualize the digital twin • Suggests DT maturity level and relevant success stories	• Discover an indicative (ROI) potential • (Optional) A CBA following ADB guideline	• Prepare and disseminate a tender/procurement document • Encapsulate Gemini Principles • Refine return on investment model	• Validate and verify through a Digital Twin Lite • Convey the value of the DT	• Scale the digital twin to other applications • Hand over the digital twin
STAKEHOLDERS	• ADB Project Team • DMC Counterparts (optional)	• ADB Project Team • DMC Counterparts • Technology Vendors (optional)	• Technology Vendors • ADB Project Team • DMC Counterparts (optional)	• ADB Project Team • DMC Counterparts • Technology Vendors	• ADB Project Team (optional) • DMC Counterparts • Technology Vendors
LEVEL OF DIGITAL TWIN UNDERSTANDING (LOW – HIGH)	◐ ○ ○	● ○ ○	● ● ●	● ● ○	● ● ●
TOOLS	Digital Twin Strategy Canvas	High-Level ROI Calculator	List of Technology Vendors	-	Digital Twin Scalability Matrix

ADB = Asian Development Bank, CBA = cost-benefit analysis, DMC = developing member country, DT = digital twin, ROI = return on investment.

Sources: The iterations in the road map were adapted from the best-practice digital twin development publications of the Centre for Digital Built Britain (CDBB), the Digital Twin Consortium, Institute of Electrical and Electronics Engineers (IEEE), Cranfield University, University of Michigan, Technical Universities (TU) Darmstadt and Ilmenau, and Deloitte.

Steps 1 to 3 of this road map are intended to help users develop the Digital Twin Lite. Steps 4 and 5 help them convey the value of the Digital Twin Lite and to consider how the Digital Twin Lite could be scaled further by the eventual asset owner and/or borrowers during the later stages of the infrastructure life cycle. The guidance provided in each of the following stages has been collated and synthesized from various sources in the digital twin ecosystem and provides industry best practices for those considering developing a digital twin.

CHECKPOINT

Before you continue with Step 1, consider this...

While digital twins are gaining industry-wide traction and have the potential to serve as a tool for developing climate-adaptive and climate-resilient infrastructure, their development can be a lengthy, complex, and expensive process. Appendix 6 contains a brief needs assessment, the results of which will also provide insights on the "gaps" that users and sponsors of the digital twin should "bridge"—either before they start or along the Digital Twin Road Map.

Step 1—Conceptualize

Through interaction with the Digital Twin Canvas, the objective of Step 1 is to help the project team conceptualize the desired solution that will be provided by a Digital Twin Lite for that specific infrastructure project.

The Digital Twin Strategy Canvas[3] incorporates elements from ADB's project proposal and documentation procedure for ease of use and serves as a planning tool the users can use to intuitively arrive at the desired solution and benefits the Digital Twin Lite should provide for the infrastructure project being assessed. This canvas will be a starting point in building and articulating a strategic case for the Digital Twin Lite, for further discussions with the primary stakeholders such as the implementing agency and technology providers (Figure 7).

Figure 7: Digital Twin Strategy Canvas

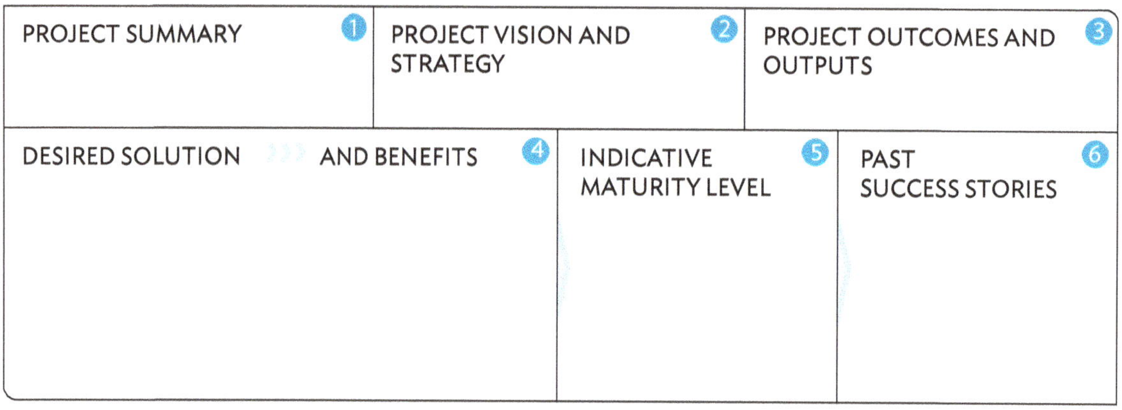

Source: Author.

As shown in Figure 7, the Digital Twin Strategy Canvas comprises the indicated sections, and should be filled in by users in successive order. To facilitate comprehension, the examples below discuss the possible application of a Digital Twin Lite as a tool in urban planning, development, and/or due diligence for Indonesia's future capital of Nusantara—to make it a sustainable, carbon-neutral city for a Nusantara Smart City (ADB 2023a). The discussion of how a Digital Twin Lite could be used to inform the development of Nusantara is a hypothetical case provided for illustrative purposes only.

1. **Project summary.** In this section, the project team is to provide a short description of the infrastructure project being considered for the digital twin, including project particulars, key objectives, stages of the project life cycle, and other key details that may be useful for other users of the canvas (e.g., procurement officers, technology vendors, officials from the implementing agency, and others). It must be noted that at this stage, the description of the project should avoid focusing on the digital twin.

[3] Earlier iterations of this canvas drew inspiration from the digital twin framework published by the Construction Innovation Hub for the Digital Twin Hub.

For example, an appropriate project summary for the Nusantara Smart City project could be:

> ***Project Summary.*** *ADB is supporting the Nusantara National Capital Authority in the development of Nusantara, the future capital city of Indonesia, as* ***a carbon-neutral forest city, to become carbon-neutral by 2045. The city of Nusantara spans 2,561 square kilometers*** *of land area and is situated on the east coast of the island of Borneo.*
>
> *The process starts with developing a "compass" in* ***planning, developing, and managing the carbon neutrality journey*** *in the form of a Net Zero Strategy. The strategy will address* ***five focus areas,*** *including Forestry and Other Land Uses (rehabilitation and protection), Energy (no fossil fuel), Industrial (green building and materials), Waste Management (circular economy), and Agriculture (regenerative agriculture).*

2. **Project vision and strategy.** This section is to identify and record important details that convey the vision and strategic relevance of the infrastructure project. This could include details of a larger regional or national strategy, or the vision of the project sponsors under which the project is a part of, and how it aligns with ADB's long-term strategy (Strategy 2030) and its operational priorities (OPs). This section of the canvas is to communicate the importance of the project to future users and key decision-makers. Once again, the vision and strategy of the project should avoid focusing on the digital twin at this stage.

   As an example, an appropriate project vision and strategy for the Nusantara Smart City project could be as follows:

   > ***Project Vision and Strategy.*** *This project is part of a wider technical assistance project aimed at supporting selected developing member countries (DMCs) to plan and develop livable cities that are smart, inclusive, environmentally sustainable, resilient, and competitive.*
   >
   > *This project greatly aligns with national strategy, as Indonesia designated Nusantara as the new capital. The project will be further supporting Indonesia's efforts (Master Plan Presidential Regulation No. 63/2022) to boost climate resilience by mitigating carbon emissions and adapting to climate change, which will pave the pathway to achieving net-zero carbon emissions in 2045.*
   >
   > *This project also supports four ADB operational priorities (OPs) such as OP3: Making Cities More Livable.*

3. **Project outputs and outcomes.** In this section, the project team begins to brainstorm the underlying question of "why" a digital twin is needed at this early stage of the infrastructure project. Using ADB's published Design and Monitoring Framework (DMF) structure, users should first identify the outcomes and outputs of their project, based on the OPs identified from the previous step (2. Project Vision and Strategy). The intended project outputs and outcomes are typically prepared by ADB project teams as part of documents, such as the project data sheet and the report and recommendation of the President, as necessary parts of the project completion report.

   For example, an appropriate Project Outcomes and Outputs for the Nusantara Smart City project could be as follows:

   > ***Project Outputs and Outcomes***
   > *Outcomes: Nusantara's capacity to plan and enforce urban planning systems, provide services, and manage finances is improved.*
   >
   > *Outputs:*
   > - *Improved urban planning systems and enforcement.*
   > - *Improved key infrastructure and municipal service delivery.*
   > - *Improved financial management systems in Nusantara, ensuring that limited financing is utilized in the most efficient manner and promoting transparency and accountability.*

At this stage, it may also be helpful to reiterate the known target outputs of the infrastructure project. For example, the Nusantara National Capital Authority published the target outputs for the Nusantara Smart City project as follows:

- *Reduce carbon emissions by 1.1 metric tons of carbon dioxide equivalent.*
- *Protect 59,000 hectares and restore 83,000 hectares of the forests to improve carbon stock.*
- *Construct 50-megawatt solar panels.*
- *60% of waste recovered and/or recycled while 40% of waste converted into energy.*

4. **Desired solution(s) and indicative benefits.** This section provides the project team with a predetermined list of potential solutions and corresponding benefits from the Digital Twin Lite, which were compiled from the analysis of various past applications recorded in the use-case library.

   By reviewing the list of desired solutions and comparing these with the project-related information in the previous sections, users are able to initially get an idea of the desired use- case for their specific project and then specify *"What will it do?"* (Figure 8). It is recommended that users select only the key or primary benefits. Alternatively, the users can simply read the list of benefits, then select the ones that would be most useful for the current challenges of the infrastructure project.

Figure 8: List of Possible Solutions and Their Corresponding Benefits

ILLUSTRATIVE

	DESIRED SOLUTION(S)...	AND INDICATIVE BENEFITS
☐	Stress test the potential infrastructure against current built-environment	Improved investment decision-making; feasibility assessment
☒	Stress test against future conditions and environments (e.g., climate change)	Improved investment decision-making; feasibility assessment; climate-resilient infrastructure
☒	Evaluate and optimize design to meet specific outcome(s)	Alternative infrastructure designs; reduce emissions and resource consumption; improved sustainability, service quality and satisfaction
☒	Urban planning tool to conceptualize different urban designs and analyze various scenarios	Improved investment decision-making; optimized land use and resource usage; improve service quality and satisfaction
☒	Collaborate and visualize virtually	Improve design process; informed and early stakeholder feedback; reduce lead time; greater access to information
☒	Immerse and experience virtually	Boost marketing potential for the digital twin; Enhance stakeholder adoption and buy-in
☐	Conduct training virtually	Improve workforce capacity; improve workplace efficiency; reduce operational lead times; improve workplace safety
☐	Monitor the construction and building of the infrastructure	Remote monitoring; real-time or near-real-time decision-making; reduce operational lead times; prevent construction delays

DESIGN → BUILD

Source: Author.

Reviewing similar digital twin use-case applications in the respective project sector (Appendix 2) could aid in a more precise recording of the desired functionality of the digital twin. The functionality described in the canvas will eventually form the basis for the functional specification document for the digital twin during its implementation.

As an example, the desired solutions and the corresponding benefits for the Nusantara Smart City could be as follows:

Examples of Digital Twin Key Benefits

	Solution	Benefit
☐	*Stress test the potential infrastructure against current built environment*	*Improved investment decision-making, enhanced feasibility assessment*
☒	*Stress test against future conditions and environments (e.g., climate change)*	*Improved investment decision-making, enhanced feasibility assessment, climate-resilient infrastructure constructed*
☒	*Evaluate and optimize design to meet specific outcome(s)*	*Alternative infrastructure designs identified; reduced emissions and resource consumption; improved sustainability, service quality, and satisfaction*
☒	*Urban planning tool to conceptualize different urban designs and analyze various scenarios*	*Improved investment decision-making, optimized land use and resource usage, improved service quality and satisfaction*
☒	*Collaborate and visualize virtually*	*Improved design process, informed and early stakeholder feedback, reduced lead time, greater access to information*
☐	*Immerse and experience virtually*	*Boosted marketing potential for the digital twin, enhanced stakeholder adoption and buy-in*
☐	*Conduct training virtually*	*Improved workforce capacity, improved workplace efficiency, reduced operational lead times, improved workplace safety*
☐	*Monitor the construction and building of the infrastructure*	*Remote monitoring enabled, real-time or near-real-time decision-making made possible, reduced operational lead times, construction delays prevented*

CHECKPOINT

How do you determine a purpose-built solution?

At this stage, if a user is unsure in selecting the appropriate solution or whether the solution proposed is purpose-built, Appendix 7 can be consulted to confirm if there is alignment between the desired solution and the underlying problem or objective it seeks to address. Also check this out: Is the Needs Assessment completed?

5. **Maturity Level.** Once the desired solutions are selected, the canvas will automatically generate the maturity level associated with the combination of functionalities (Figure 9). Details on the maturity levels can be revisited in Section 1.5, nonetheless, the canvas provides brief descriptions of the selected maturity level in response to two key questions: "What can it do?" and "What does it need?"

Figure 9: Autogenerated Maturity Level

Level 3: Predictive Twin

What can it do?

In addition to the asset(s) visualized on a virtual plain, through the use of advanced analytics and integration of real-time and historic data, the Predictive Twin is able to generate answers to 'what if' questions personalized and tailored to each unique asset(s), thereby providing unique and valuable insights.

What does it need?

This 'predictive' capability may come from these enabling technologies:

Artificial Intelligence (AI)
AI and branches of AI, allow analytics to incorporate larger volumes of data

Internet of Things (IoT)
IoT allows the collection of real-time data specific to the asset(s), allowing tailored analysis

Source: Author.

6. **Success Stories.** Based on the indicative maturity level, the canvas will provide suggestions from past digital twin application cases for additional information and references. Each of the suggested case studies will provide information on the objectives of the digital twin, relevant ADB sector, technology provider, primary application, project location and duration, and relevant software or technology involved. More examples of the relevant maturity level can be further sourced from the use-case library (Figure 10).

Figure 10: Autogenerated List of Past Success Stories

Digital Twin Past Success Stories

Level 3

Digital Twin of Siemensstadt Square
Virtual Singapore
New South Wales (NSW) Spatial Digital Twin
Digital Twin of Monaco
Digital Twin Victoria
Penang Smart Mobility
Digital Twin of a Wastewater Treatment Plant - Echowater
Digital Twin of a Hydraulic Pipe System in Ayodhya
Digital Twin for Road Design - Uzbekistan A380
Digital Twin of Rail Crossings - Parkdale

Source: A screenshot of the "Success Stories" section in the DT Strategy Canvas and ROI Calculator tool.

Users are encouraged to read these case studies as it will further consolidate the details surrounding the Digital Twin Lite for their own infrastructure project.

Step 2: Business Case

With the Digital Twin Strategy Canvas at Step 1 completed, users should now have a foundational understanding of the proposed digital twin solution design—that is, its expected functionality, maturity level, benefits, and purpose (the problem–solution alignment). However, the question of whether users and sponsors should develop the full-scale digital twin remains.

The Business Case provides a preliminary answer to this question by evaluating the indicative return on investment (ROI)—an outcome-based approach to understand and evaluate the expected net socioeconomic value of the digital twin. To help ensure the efficient use of development funds, this ROI analysis should be conducted in accordance with core ADB guidelines, such as the *Guidelines for the Economic Analysis of Projects*, or the *Cost–Benefit Analysis for Development* documents. At this stage, the business case would further complement the work of project teams in the preparation of documents, such as project data sheets.

Based on the best practice example, the business case is recommended to be divided into two parts and completed with the help of a specialized consultant (see also Appendix 8 and Appendix 9). The first part is to build a **Technical Case** that elaborates on the data, IT (software and hardware), and other technical requirements of the proposed digital twin solution (enabling technologies). The second part is the integration of the technical case to build an **Investment Case** that provides a high-level assessment of the financial requirements (capital expenses, operating expenses, and other expenses) and tangible and/or intangible benefits of the proposed digital twin solution.

This framework instead makes use of a high-level digital twin **ROI Calculator**, supported by the Digital Twin Use-Case Library and Strategy Canvas, to provide this indicative estimation. Anchored on its data, further update of the evolving use-case library will increase the accuracy of the ROI calculator's numbers. This ROI calculator will guide the project teams in estimating the costs of a digital twin by exploring the scale of the underlying infrastructure asset and estimating the benefits by providing suggested cost savings toward initial project capital. Project teams should use the ROI Calculator as a tool for this high-level analysis, which could be beneficial as talking points in discussions with DMCs or other clients.

The possible application of a digital twin solution for Indonesia's future sustainable, smart-city capital of Nusantara from Step 1 can continue to be used as a case study.

Step 2.1 Cost Estimations for the Digital Twin

Use the ROI Calculator to estimate the high-level costs of the digital twin. This will be calculated based on available investment cost data from precedent use-cases for a digital twin with similar size and functionalities. Answer the questions *"What is the size of the underlying Physical Twin?"* and *"How complex does the digital twin need to be given the desired functionalities?"* The indicative cost of the digital twin scales accordingly to these two criteria:

- **Infrastructure asset scale.** This reflects the general size of the underlying asset or "Physical Twin" serving as a base for the digital twin. The ROI Calculator provides three asset scale options for users to select from —small, medium, and large (Figure 11). Each option represents a different number of assets being digitized within or across sectors, and consequently, the size and cost of the digitalization efforts. Though this categorization is inherently subjective (not based on measurements like square meters), it can scale on both size and count of the asset. For instance, while a road may be a singular asset (hence, small scale), if that road is 1,000-kilometer long then it may be more appropriately categorized as a medium-scale asset.

Figure 11: Illustrative Scale of the Infrastructure Assets

1. Small-scale assets
Typically projects comprising a single infrastructure asset.

<u>For example:</u> Building, bridge, road, power plant, etc.

2. Medium-scale assets
Typically projects comprising multiple infrastructure assets.

<u>For example:</u> Campus, solar farm, wind farm, etc.

3. Large-scale assets
Typically projects comprising multiple infrastructure assets across sectors, citywide or nationwide.

<u>For example:</u> Virtual Singapore, road system of a country, large cities, etc.

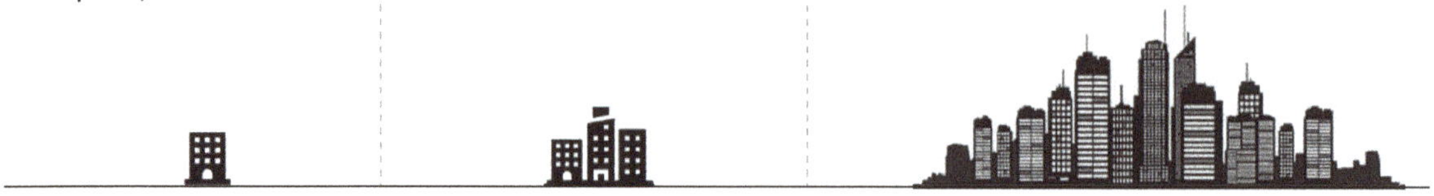

Source: Author.

- **Indicative maturity level.** This involves the proposed Digital Twin Maturity Level (Levels 1–5) assigned to the desired solution to reflect the level of complexity, functionality, and technology required. Increasing complexity requires additional hardware and software and, hence, translates to higher cost of development. This input will be automatically suggested by the Digital Twin Strategy Canvas and carried through to the ROI Calculator.

Using these two inputs, the ROI Calculator will fetch a statistically analyzed cost data point from the information available in the Use-Case Library that matches the required criteria (Figure 12). As an option, users can consider the variation within this data through scenarios that increase or decrease the cost values through one standard deviation of the respective data. An optimistic scenario will consider a lower digital twin cost, and vice versa, for a pessimistic scenario.

Figure 12: Range of Digital Twin Costs

Range of Digital Twin cost based on selected Maturity Level and Scale of Asset*

<u>Remarks about the range:</u>

Given that the default value for the indicative cost of the digital twin implementation will be the median cost. Project team members will also have the option to select the minimum and maximum cost for their respective digital twin configuration. The selected value will be used in the ROI calculation.

**The minimum and maximum range is derived from the Standard Deviation of all cost for each Asset Scale under each Maturity Level.*

Min = Optimistic; Median = Conservative; Max = Pessimistic

[OPTIONAL] Selected cost:

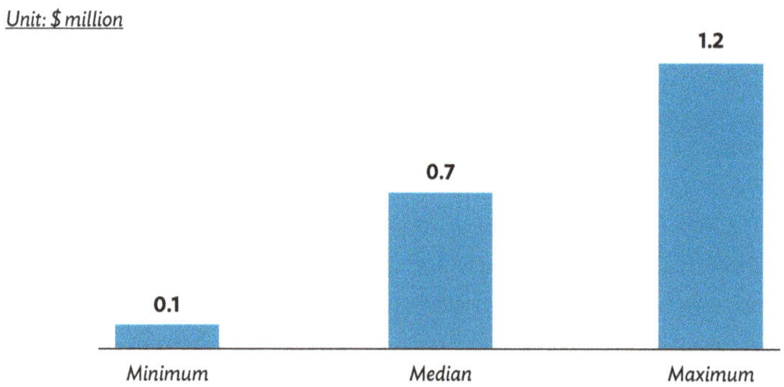

Note: The Return on Investment (ROI) Calculator interactive interface on digital twin benefit data variance was based on use-cases.
Source: Author.

While costs may range from $100,000 to over $10 million, organizations often spend over $1 million to develop and operate a full-scale digital twin, and below or around $1 million to develop a Digital Twin Lite. The ROI Calculator's suggestions can range from $100,000 to $1.2 million for a Level 1 small-scale digital twin, and $19 million to $31 million for a Level 3 city-scale digital twin.

Technological alternatives and quotations can also cause price differentials. For example, using platform as a service (PaaS), cloud environments with necessary tools to build and operate an application (such as IoT TwinMaker by Amazon Web Services [AWS], Azure Digital Twins, and Bentley iTwin Platform), can lower up-front costs for the twin, but increase operational costs. In general, platform prices in Southeast Asia are typically 30% higher than in the United States and 8% higher than in the European Union.

An example of costs for a potential digital twin for Nusantara could be as follows:

High-level cost estimate example:

- ***Infrastructure asset scale.*** *Large-scale asset (a city-scale asset for a large, smart-city capital across 200 hectares for their phase 2 development focused on mixed-use areas)*
- ***Indicative maturity level.*** *Maturity Level 3, a Predictive Twin (provided by the calculator and canvas, corresponding to the desired solution and benefits)*
- ***High-level cost of digital twin:*** *$25 million for a Level 3, large-scale asset twin*

Project teams may already have some estimate on the cost for their digital twin through vendor engagements, or by determining high-level financial requirements using ADB's publication on *Cost Estimation in Sovereign Operations* as a guide (Appendix 8). In these instances, the ROI calculator provides an **override** to replace suggested indicative cost values as an option.

Step 2.2 Benefit Estimations of the Digital Twin

Users should continue using the ROI Calculator to estimate the high-level benefits of the digital twin, calculated as a function of cost savings from the total estimated capital expenditure of the underlying infrastructure project. This is based on generalized percentages applied to project expenses. Accordingly, users should consider the following inputs:

- **Estimated capital expenditures (CAPEX)** represent a field for users to populate the total capital costs for the underlying project's infrastructure asset (not the digital twin and/or Digital Twin Lite to be built). The best CAPEX estimate for infrastructure assets should come from project teams or the DMC to populate this input.
- **Indicative benefits** reflect a list of pre-determined key benefit categories derived from what similar precedent use-cases have achieved. These are benefits that have been quantified in either percentages or absolute dollar values (e.g., cost savings of 15% or $200,000) based on the potential twin's maturity level. After users complete the "Desired solution(s) and key benefits" quadrant of the Digital Twin Strategy Canvas, this field is automatically populated with the corresponding benefits for those choices.

  Categories of Key Benefits

  - Visualization and monitoring
  - Informed decision-making
  - Resource optimization and loss reduction
  - Productivity gains
  - Improved operations, inspection, and maintenance
  - Improved or optimized financial performance
  - Improved quality

- Increased customer satisfaction
- Improved knowledge and collaboration
- Security and safety
- Predictive intelligence
- Risk management and resilience
- Improved environmental sustainability

- **Estimated carbon emissions (optional)** provide users with an additional aisle to calculate emission reduction benefits based on the social cost of carbon (International Foundation for Impacts, Inc. and Value Balancing Alliance 2024). The ROI Calculator will translate the total estimated carbon emissions produced over the entire project's life cycle into indicative US dollar impact—reflecting carbon reductions as a result of implementing the digital twin.

Users can also consider the variation within the analyzed precedent data, which was used to adjust the benefit percentage applied toward CAPEX by one standard deviation. The variation can change depending on the associated key benefits under consideration (Figure 13).

Figure 13: Range of Digital Twin Benefits

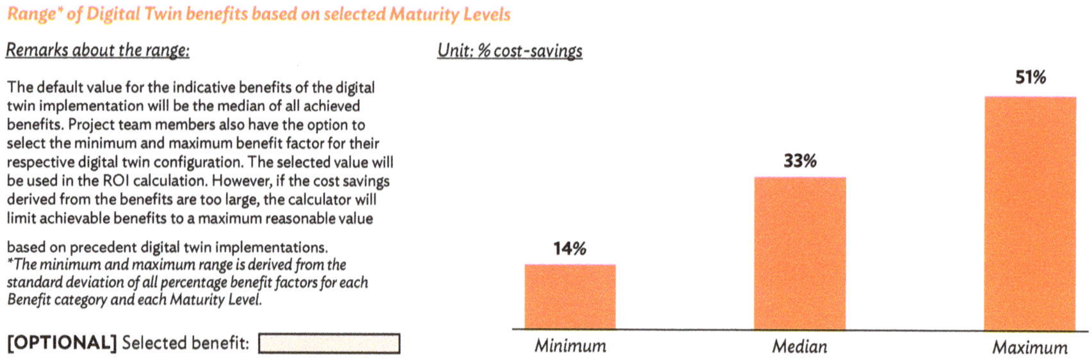

Note: The Return on Investment (ROI) Calculator interactive interface on digital twin benefit data variance was based on use-cases.
Source: Author.

As an example, the indicative benefits of a potential digital twin for Nusantara could be as follows:

Example of a High-Level Cost Estimate

- ***Estimated CAPEX:*** *$846 million (the estimated cost for Phase 2 of the Nusantara Project from 2025 to 2029, which is focused on the construction of mixed-use areas)*
- ***Indicative benefits:*** *The potential digital twin for Nusantara can achieve the following:*

  ☒ *Visualization and monitoring (Qualitative)*
  ☒ *Informed decision-making (Qualitative)*
  ☒ *Productivity gains (Median: 50%)*
  ☐ *Improved operations, inspection, and maintenance*
  ☒ *Improved or optimized financial performance (Median: 33%)*
  ☒ *Improve environmental sustainability (Median: 40%) and others.*

- *High-Level Benefits of Digital Twin: $100 million for a design-and-built project with 12 key benefits*

As in costs, project teams may already have some estimate on the total US dollar benefits to be achieved by the digital twin. This could be by manually quantifying the economic prices of benefits through referring to ADB's *Guidelines for the Economic Analysis of Projects*, which details the method for valuing project benefits in major sectors of ADB operations. The ROI Calculator provides an override to replace suggested indicative benefit estimates as an option.

CHECKPOINT

Does the business case need a detailed breakdown?

At this stage, should a user desire to build a more complex business case driven by best practice, Appendix 8 can be consulted further to guide the overall process. In general, best practice business case should perform a detailed bottom-up analysis of the technical (enabling technologies) and business requirements (quantified value-added benefits). This analysis is recommended to be completed with the help of a specialized technology vendor or consultant.

Users are recommended to complete these four inputs within the tool (minimum of two, excluding automatic population through the Digital Twin Strategy Canvas) to perform a high-level estimation for a best-suited digital twin at full scale. However, to estimate more accurately the ROI and scope in the calculation for a full-scale digital twin or a Digital Twin Lite, it is recommended that a specialized consultant who can give a detailed breakdown and quote be engaged. A Digital Twin Lite should be pursued if the ROI is greater than 120% to 125% in general. The **indicative ROI potential for Nusantara's Digital Twin solution is 400%, which is an example of a high-level ROI potential.**

Step 3: Procure and Build

If you have reached this stage, it means that the digital twin opportunity presents an optimistic ROI figure, as highlighted in Step 2. It also indicates that it makes financial and strategic sense to pursue its implementation.

As the next step, the details and feasibility of the digital twin must evolve with the help and collaboration of technology experts. The objective of Step 3 is to comprehensively guide vendor engagement and selection through a tendering process. This step will also recommend international frameworks to be observed throughout the development of a digital twin. This ensures that the digital twin procured is effective while retaining sufficient safeguards required for a public infrastructure service.

Prior to continuing Step 3, however, it may be important for relevant stakeholders to engage and reach a consensus on the legal and commercial aspects. This will depend on the scope and scale of the digital twin under consideration. For instance, a digital twin requiring the collection and processing of personal data will require certain protocols to be factored into the design. For such purposes, ADB's **internal divisions specializing in technology implementations may be consulted**, such as the Digital Technology for Development division. The process may further reveal the desired or required level of involvement from the sponsors or hosts of the infrastructure project.

CHECKPOINT

Before you continue to Step 3, consider this...

- **Has the indicative investment case been built?**

Users should not proceed to Step 3 without having completed a high-level investment case, considering the associated business and technical requirements of the digital twin. Understanding these elements at minimum will allow better alignment with the potential technical provider and manage the expectations of involved stakeholders. Reviewing and disseminating potential costs and benefits to stakeholders can further increase buy-in.

- **Does the investment case achieve acceptable returns?**

The final cost-benefit or ROI analysis results may deviate from expectations. Revisit initial defined functionalities and benefits in the Digital Twin Strategy Canvas, and the assumptions used to ensure the feasibility and comprehensiveness of the analysis and the twin. This may reveal if the digital twin remains a plausible solution for the high-value problem and purpose, or if procurement should commence with risks, if any.

- **Should a specialized, external consultant be engaged?**

Given the scarcity of comprehensive guidelines regarding digital twin ROI calculations and limited availability of metrics for quantifiable outcomes, engaging a specialized consultant may be required to aid in estimating a more accurate ROI and scoping the calculation for a Digital Twin Lite.

The terms of reference (TOR) is a document aimed at communicating the needs and benefits of the contemplated digital twin. At the end of the procurement phase, the accepted proposal should clearly describe the composition of the digital twin and the technologies involved, the phases of implementation, and other details that are involved in the successful delivery and continued use of the digital twin.

The TOR should contain the following three key components:

1. **Objective and Purpose**

   Following the elements of the Digital Twin Strategy Canvas formulated in Step 1, the TOR should thoroughly elaborate on the various details to describe the context, the details of the infrastructure project, the overarching objective of the Digital Twin Lite, and its expected outputs.

   As an example, the overarching objective of the Digital Twin Lite for the Nusantara Smart City could read:

   > **Objective of the Digital Twin Lite:**
   >
   > ADB approved the project in response to a government request. The objective is to equip the city **with a digital twin ecosystem to visualize and simulate large-scale impacts on the city**. Through the project, the city seeks to identify which infrastructure or building requires immediate attention and that may be upgraded to achieve net-zero carbon emissions within a specified timeline.

Outputs expected of the Digital Twin Lite:

The project has three outputs:

(i) 3D geometrical models on a timeline module, which was created to allow the user to quickly set a date and time while exposing the ability to "play" through the timed intervals.
(ii) Sustainability impact of infrastructure and building that hold certain data, both static and data-based.
(iii) Ability to show and chart graphs to visually identify data patterns as well as the inclusion of transport routes, cycle routes, and other public points of interest.

Where possible, if additional services are needed for the successful adoption of the digital twin, the tender should specify such nontechnical requirements. For example, if there is limited technical expertise at the implementing agency, the project may require capacity-building or training workshops to ensure a successful handover.

At this stage, the tender could suggest a possible technology configuration of the digital twins that may be expected of the vendor or a consortium of vendors to deliver these services. For instance, a project that expects to apply machine learning to analyze traffic patterns may potentially require joint bids.

2. **Scope of the Assignment, Deliverables, Payment Schedule, and Timeline**

Building from sections 4, 5, and 6 of the canvas, the TOR should describe the scope and desired solution of the Digital Twin Lite and the indicative maturity level. To ensure that the TOR is comprehensive and aligned with best practices, users can draw inspiration from the scope of comparable digital twin success stories that are available in the use-case library.

As an example, the scope of the assignment for the Nusantara Smart City could read:

Scope of the Assignment:

The consultant firm engaged under this assignment will undertake the following tasks:

(i) **Understand the delineation of boundaries for the city.** Geographical coverage needs to be precise and factors such as administrative divisions, neighborhoods, and sites need to be clarified. The initial focus of the digital twin implementation will be on strategically identified areas within Nusantara City, addressing immediate urban challenges and development needs.
(ii) **Define the functionalities and features.** Specific functional and nonfunctional features of the digital twin is required. Features such as real-time monitoring, predictive modeling, scenario analysis, and other visualization functionality need to be considered. Also, nonfunctional requirements such as usability, user interface, connectivity in remote locations, and others need to be identified as part of the scope.
(iii) **Identify the stakeholders.** Identifying key stakeholders, departments, and communities involved in the project is equally important. This includes people who will be directly or indirectly impacted as a result of the project on which the digital twin will be built.
(iv) **Develop the 3D digital twin model.** The firm will develop the 3D digital twin model with the necessary predictive capabilities within 12 months of the commencement of the assignment. The 3D digital twin model should be capable of visually simulating the impacts of climate events over the next 100 years and help in identifying the potential upgrades, retrofits, and additions to the existing infrastructure to obtain net-zero targets.

Make sure to ask the technology vendor (Appendix 9 for a potential list of technology providers) to (i) conduct a "technical analysis;" (ii) get clarity on data availability and integrity; (iii) understand data gaps; and (iv) to know how data will be collected, migrated, transformed, and protected during the use the Digital Twin Lite. By examining these aspects, the vendor can provide a clear picture of the existing data landscape, highlight potential challenges (Appendix 1), and propose strategies to ensure data reliability and security. Digital twins are built on sensitive data and its interconnectivity with other systems within the natural built environment imposes risks related to data breaches. Therefore, it is important to address these risks in order to maintain the integrity, availability, and confidentiality of the digital twin.

As an example, the technical analysis portion of the TOR for the Nusantara Smart City could read as follows:

> The consultant firm will build the required datasets that will:
>
> 1. Provide synthetic data made for the Bureau of Statistics, which will include resources within Indonesia.
> 2. Create new 3D geospatial models that are included within a specific area.
> 3. Extract the IoT sensors and edge data through traffic; ensure that pedestrian movements are collated, cleansed, and ingested within the digital twin platform.
> 4. Enable the prediction of various modeling across the entire site.
> 5. Engage with stakeholders and determine user acceptance testing, including user interface functionalities and features.
>
> ** Note that data cleansing is required for all data collated.*
>
> The intended use-case is for the Nusantara government to be able to make informed decisions on the status of the city in order to achieve a zero-emission city within a specified time frame. This requires government officials to make informed decisions on all the buildings and to see which ones are consuming excess amounts of energy, water, and with a high carbon output.

If additional technical guidance is needed for scoping, a technology vendor could assist with a discovery phase, which should last around 2–4 weeks. During this period, the vendor works closely with the project team to understand the specific requirements and constraints of your project. They will assess the current technological infrastructure, evaluate potential solutions, and provide recommendations for the Digital Twin Lite's implementation. This discovery phase is designed to gather detailed insights and develop a tailored approach that aligns with the organization's objectives, ensuring that the subsequent development and deployment phases proceed smoothly and effectively.

The TOR further needs to communicate clear deliverables, payment schedule, and timeline. The primary stakeholders of the project should be consulted to confirm the required deliverables, and this may differ from project to project. However, it is recommended that the following elements be included in the deliverables:

(i) **Knowledge portion**—to share the digital twin and/or Digital Twin Lite findings with other projects team (in ADB and/or DMC).
(ii) **Cost-benefit analysis for the Digital Twin Lite**—to validate the Digital Twin Lite in Step 4 of the road map.
(iii) **Technical report**—to be used in Step 5 of the road map, if the Digital Twin Lite is handed over to another party.

The budget and timeline for the Digital Twin Lite can be discretionary, but ideally, it should cost less than $1 million and be deployed in less than 1 year in most cases.

As an example, a table for deliverables and payment for the Nusantara Smart City project is presented in Table 3.

Table 3: Deliverables and Payment Schedules

Deliverable	Description	Due date from NTP	Payment Schedule
Gap analysis	Gap analysis conducted during the creation of the digital twin shall be addressed as part of the follow-on actions upon completion of the MVP.	2 months	$250,000
Detailed technical proposal	Data governance and management will be outlined as part of the proposal, including applications systems and software. A complete management framework is required to ensure complete sovereignty of systems and data.	4 months	$500,000
Recommendation and road map	A viable working road map that considers all the necessary commercial, financial, and implementation plan is created.	6 months	$750,000
Minimum viable product	Minimum viable product is developed that will show a working product with minimum functionality. Hence, the functional requirement will be lower.	12 months	$1.5 million
Rollout of preliminary production	Preliminary production will have the functional requirements and the user interface upgraded as more features and functions are added.	24 months	$3 million
Industrialized rollout	Industrialized rollout provides a viable product to be used across multiple different stakeholders.	36 months	$4.5 million

MVP = minimum viable product, NTP = notice to proceed.
Source: Adapted from Aurecon's terms of reference for the digital twin development.

The TOR should further indicate that the DMC project teams will have access to and own the Digital Twin Lite (including its licenses, code, data models and/or lakes, and others) at the end of the development.

3. **Other Industry Best Practices**

   This section is an optional but recommended portion of the TOR. The project teams should require consultants to meet certain qualification requirements, such as a minimum number of years of experience working with related technologies of digital twins. Also, considering the protocols proposed by the consultants for data security and other safeguards would be integral to having a functional but safe Digital Twin Lite.

   A. Security Requirements

   The tender should dedicate a section that describes the measures for cybersecurity and privacy protection, which will prevent potential threats to data integrity, unauthorized access, and malware.

Some examples of cybersecurity measures for consideration are as follows:

- **Data encryption**—A data encryption software will ensure that information exchanged between the digital twin and the physical entity, as well as the data stored in the twin or cloud system, are unreadable by users who do not have access. Having an authentication procedure also adds another layer of verification for the user's identity, preventing unauthorized access to the system.
- **Access control and auditing system**—The deployment of an access control and auditing system will define and enforce who can access and modify the digital twin. Having a standard auditing protocol in place enables tracking and recording of activities related to the digital twin, such as data transfers, security incidents, and configuration changes.
- **Security updates—**Deploying regular security updates and patches will maintain the integrity of the digital twin security system by eliminating vulnerabilities, fixing bugs, or errors that can lead to cybersecurity threats.
- **Training protocols**—These protocols for users and staff will regularly interact, operate, and maintain the digital twin system on the best practices, policies, and procedures of security. This also includes raising awareness on the potential cybersecurity risks and the consequences of using the digital twin.

In addition, the following data security standards and frameworks may be considered:

- ISO/IEC JTC1/SC 27—Information security, cybersecurity, and privacy protection: Addresses the security requirements of capturing data and managing information, such as security management systems and security processes.
- 2021 ISO TC184/SC4—Industrial data: Ensures the standardization of the content, meaning, structure and representation, and quality management of the information required to define a product.
- ISO 10303—Industrial automation systems and integration: Also known as STEP (Standard for the Exchange of Product model data), it provides a standard for the representation and exchange of product data.
- ISO 15926—Integration of life-cycle data for process plants, including oil and gas production facilities: Specifies a standard for the integration, sharing, exchange, and handover of information throughout the life cycle of a facility.
- ISO 14306—Defines standardized 3D CAD data exchange format in the context of industrial automation systems and integration,
- ISO/PAS 17506—Industrial automation systems and integration–Collaborative Design Activity (COLLADA) digital asset schema specification: Specifies the COLLADA file format, which is used to ensure compatibility and interchangeability of digital assets in industrial automation systems.

B. Other Safeguards and Requirements

The tender should contain an expanded list of the safeguards and principles that must be adhered to in designing, commissioning, testing, and in the continued use of the digital twin. This encompasses compliance with both internal and external guidelines of ADB.

At a minimum, the Gemini Principles should be considered. The Gemini Principles were created by the Centre for Digital Built Britain to aid in the development of a National Digital Twin of the United Kingdom. It ensures that the digital twin is functional, trustworthy, and useful. There are nine principles under these three main pillars—**purpose, trust, and function**. The principles are also descriptive and applicable to all solutions, which encourages flexibility for innovation and development. The Gemini Principles are covered in more detail in Appendix 10.

Step 4: Assess

By interacting with the Digital Twin Lite itself during and after its development, the following objective will ensure that it is purpose-built and meets initial objectives. This involves a constant and thorough assessment of the Digital Twin Lite.

Assessment is typically a recurring two-step approach, done through **verifying** the Digital Twin Lite against functionality, and **validating** it against business case requirements until added value is achieved. The project team must work together with the technology provider to authenticate and align with two prior inputs to answer the following questions: *"Does the Digital Twin Lite align with and perform the strategy and solutions mapped out in the Digital Twin Strategy Canvas?"* and *"Does the Digital Twin Lite deliver targeted business benefit and achieve a similar ROI as estimated in the Business Case?"*

Verification and validation will synthesize the data collected throughout the development, implementation, and operations while being informed by Steps 1 and 2 to perform this evaluation.

Step 4.1 Verify

Verification, in essence, tests and determines if the Digital Twin Lite addresses the problem and needs set by the objectives, and that it functions well. The project team's goals should be to interact with and experience the developed Digital Twin Lite to ensure it is satisfactory and to determine whether it meets the specified requirements, performs reliably, and is secure.

While the criteria for verification can vary significantly based on project context, team necessities, and the specific forms and configurations the Digital Twin Lite takes, it can be generally tested for three primary fields: its **functionality, usability, and reliability**.

- **Functionality.** This determines if the Digital Twin Lite does what it is intended to do. A recommended approach is to refer to the Digital Twin Strategy Canvas (Step 1) and determine if the desired solutions and benefits (qualitative) are reflected by checking if the Digital Twin Lite meets the users' needs. Project teams should also regularly interact with the twin. This can be done by integrating the project team's data into the Digital Twin Lite to see if it functions well under specific conditions, like user loads or network speeds. This also involves testing if it works across various users' systems, devices, or other software and hardware components to ensure interoperability. For instance, check if a construction monitoring twin crashes when terabytes of drone and satellite data are imported in.
- **Usability.** This determines the ease of the overall Digital Twin Lite's user experience. The user interface should be experienced by the various potential users to identify potential gaps or deficiencies. These gaps can then be subsequently addressed through either further bug-fixing and development, or by training the potential users by the technology vendor.
- **Output and reliability.** This determines if the output and solution are of quality. Through use of the solution and testing or by simulating its different outputs, project teams should identify their satisfaction levels or if there is a need for better solutions. To test reliability, it is recommended that stress tests be performed to see if the solution is safe and consistent over time without failures, crashes, or downtime. This may also involve alignment of the digital twin with standards and principles (refer to Step 3 and Gemini Principles in Appendix 10). Running the Digital Twin Lite with and without certain data inputs can additionally help determine its reliance on certain data needs or bottlenecks.

Step 4.2 Validate

After verifying the Digital Twin Lite, project teams should next aim to assess if it meets its intended purpose. Validation determines if the Digital Twin Lite will or is producing acceptable benefits and returns initially hypothesized at a certain cost to reflect a full-scale implementation of a digital twin. This is done through analysis of both qualitative and quantitative elements based on the desired benefits from Step 1, and the ROI estimation from Step 2.

Again, the purpose of developing and assessing a Digital Twin Lite is to inform the possibilities of maximized returns and value through a smaller scope and lower financial commitment (Box 3). The Digital Twin Lite should be envisioned to be iterated upon and developed progressively to maximize ROI. Project teams are recommended to test the initial ROI against partial assumptions by breaking down benefit and cost elements. Working with technology vendors, validate the Digital Twin Lite with the following considerations:

- **Cost of the Digital Twin Lite.** This aims to answer the question *"Does the estimated cost match the actual cost of the Digital Twin Lite by itself and when scaled?"* In this comparison, project teams should use the costs provided by the selected technology vendor based on procurement documents. Alternatively, consulting engaged vendors to provide cost quotes for a full-scale digital twin implementation can also be done.
- **Total benefits quantified.** This partial assumption asks, *"Does the quantified benefits align with the estimated benefits in the business case?"* During the operations of the Digital Twin Lite, any benefit achieved should be noted and quantified for analysis. Note that the benefits achieved may not be of a similar magnitude (e.g., save $2 million in costs) but could be of similar proportions (e.g., save 20% in costs). This comparison allows for evaluating and addressing discrepancies that may arise. For example, if the assumed benefit of 10% emission reductions from design are unachieved, determine and implement potential fixes through further analysis.
- **Return on investment (ROI).** The final consideration asks, *"Does the new ROI maintain similar results to initially estimated returns?"* Project teams are recommended to recalculate a new ROI figure based on the new costs and benefits resulting from the Digital Twin Lite to compare with estimates. ADB's *Cost–Benefit Analysis for Development* can be used as a reference throughout this entire process. Otherwise, support from the technology vendor can be warranted to perform this analysis, like in ADB's Digital Twins in Road Design for Uzbekistan's A380 Highway project with the company ORIS.

Box 3: Possible Digital Twin Lite Development Approaches

It is possible that the development of the Digital Twin Lite may take one of two forms: a benefit-driven approach or a cost-driven approach.

The **benefit-driven approach** may seek to answer this: *"To achieve the following benefits, how much will it cost, and what are the practical returns?"* This sets static the desired benefits (perhaps scaled down to be indicative of the full-scale implementation) to determine the actual cost of achieving them. This may reveal realistic cost expectations for certain return requirements.

The **cost-driven approach** asks the question *'With the following budget, what benefits and returns can the Digital Twin practically realize?'* This seeks to determine what benefits can be realistically obtained given a budget constraint and still maintain an acceptable return on investment. This may reveal costs to be allocated towards benefits that can provide the most value for money.

Source: Author.

The resulting ROI of the Digital Twin Lite can be indicative of the full-scale deployment of the digital twin. A positive Digital Twin Lite ROI will likely result in a positive ROI for the full-scale digital twin, validating initial assumptions. However, this may be more relevant for "quick-win" scaling along similar configurations (Step 5). A negative pilot ROI can reveal the ineffectiveness or the inefficiency in the current configuration. This mitigates the risk of implementing an expensive and unoptimized digital twin for the entire project and allowing changes to be made.

As an option, validation of an otherwise full-scale deployment of a digital twin can be tested directly against its initial ROI assumptions. Measuring and comparing real performance data to the hypothesis will reveal areas of improvement. Adjust and tune the digital twin as necessary to best reflect the ideal state in the model.

After verification and validation, it is suggested that the proof of value realized from the Digital Twin Lite be communicated to acquire further buy-in from relevant agencies involved.

CHECKPOINT

Before you continue to Step 5, consider this...

- **Has the developed Digital Twin Lite been fully verified and validated?**

Users should not proceed to Step 5 before thoroughly assessing if the current Digital Twin Lite is achieving the desired outcomes and benefits. Issues or errors in the current system (though continuously treated through maintenance) are likely to increase costs down the line. Continue engaging a technical provider until goals are met or revisit key solutions, functionalities, and desired benefits in Steps 1–2.

- **Has the technical provider formally confirmed that the Digital Twin Lite is ready to begin formal operations or be scaled?**

Although the Digital Twin Lite may pass verification and validation standards, it may not have the proper digital infrastructure to be scaled in size or complexity. It is recommended that a technical provider be consulted to assist in this process and ensure future-proofing.

- **Is there conviction that project stakeholders have or will have the knowledge, capacity to operate, or maintain the Digital Twin Lite?**

Do the ultimate users of the Digital Twin Lite have adequate proficiency and are comfortable in operating the Digital Twin with minimal assistance? Consider the use of training workshops or operational manuals, as well as user interaction and testing of the system.

Step 5: Scale

The final stage will explore opportunities to scale the digital twin and identify ways in which additional value can be realized through scaling. At this stage, the digital twin implementation in Step 4, whether in the form of a pilot or full-scale deployment, should have demonstrated success metrics addressing the objectives outlined in Step 1 thereby validating the benefits and costs identified in Step 2.

Step 5.1 Scaling the Digital Twin Lite

The digital twin journey should be treated as an ongoing initiative that extends beyond the identification, deployment, and realization of benefits—emphasizing continuity and sustained operational enhancements. Thus, it is important to continue capitalizing on these benefits and eventually scale the digital twin to other applications, making changes to the digital twins and observing success metrics to create the best possible configuration. Ultimately, there should be continued engagement with a consultant or technology provider to adopt an iterative approach to accelerate learning, proactively manage risks, and maximize the return on initial investments.

The decision to scale digital twins is contingent to the success of *Step 4* and should target adjacent opportunities and extend to other elements associated with the underlying project. The key considerations for scaling a digital twin can be summarized into the following scalability matrix (Figure 14).

Figure 14: Digital Twin Scalability Matrix

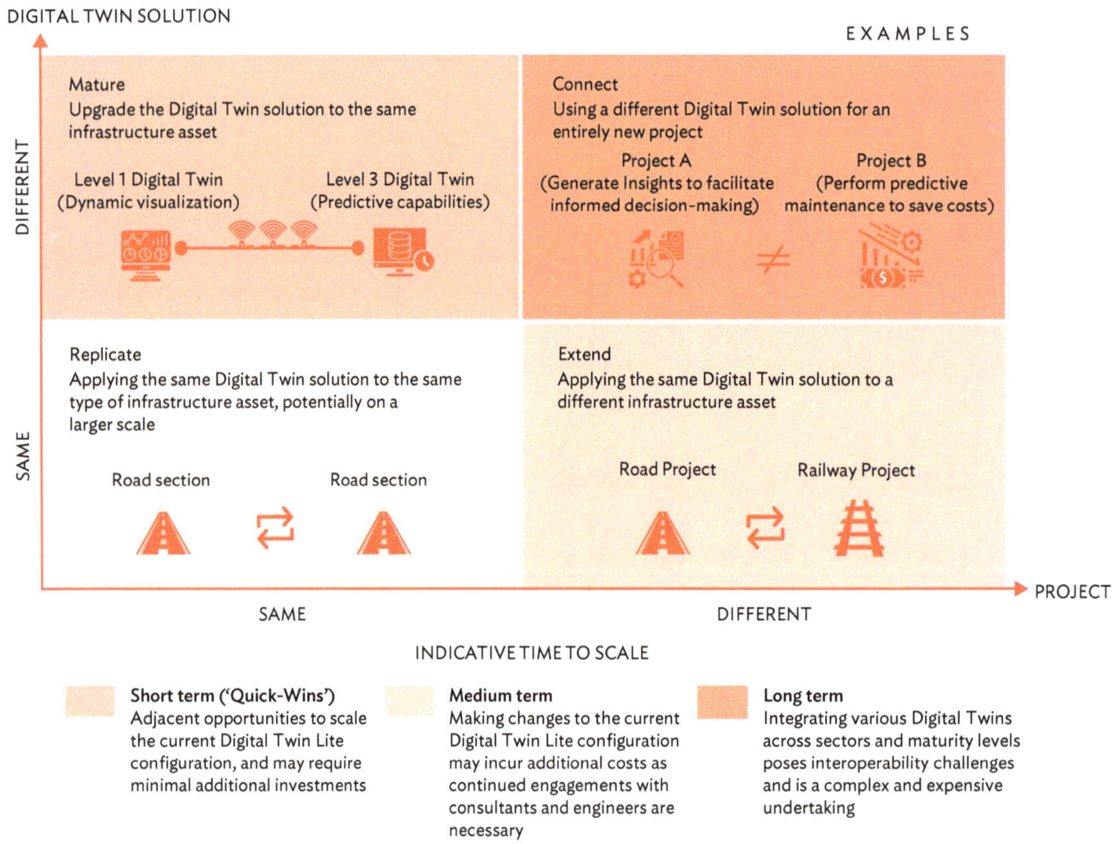

Source: Author.

1. **Extend**

The decision to extend a digital twin can be made based on the assumption that the current configuration will be applied to the same project with minimal changes to meet those project requirements. Extending the current configuration means deploying a full-scale digital twin that encompasses the entire system, which comes naturally after implementing the pilot phase. For example, the pilot phase digital twin for monitoring two wind turbines can be extended to an entire wind farm.

2. **Replicate**

Alternatively, applying the same digital twin configuration can also be considered for a different project with similar objectives. Replicating the current configuration can significantly save costs as it will not require major reconfigurations to meet the requirements of the project. Undergoing additional consultation and engineering engagements will not be necessary, and investing in additional technology enablers can be deemed optional. Scaling through replication is another instance where quick wins can be capitalized, maximizing returns, and capturing adjacent opportunities. For example, a digital twin built for roads during the planning and design phase can be applied to railway projects as both objectives lead to optimizing resource allocation and maximizing efficiency.

Before replicating the current digital twin configuration to a different project:

Consider the scope of the underlying project in Step 1 to assess similarities under each component of the "Digital Twin Strategy Canvas" that forms the problem statement.

1. *Understand the thematic problems of the underlying project—Is it climate-related, or operational (resource and cost optimization)?*
2. *Make a hypothesis on the digital twin functionality to address the thematic problems—Is the maturity level and corresponding features suitable for the project?*
3. *Expect improvements from deploying digital twins—Can the high-level metrics from the current configuration be applied to the new project?*

3. **Mature**

In cases where a digital twin is applied to different aspects of the same project, a new digital twin configuration may be considered to address a new set of objectives. Designing a new configuration may involve changing the complexity levels of the existing digital twin, using the current configuration as a foundation to expand its capabilities by integrating new technology enablers such as artificial intelligence (AI). However, increasing the complexity of a digital twin will not necessitate new project applications as the foundational configuration will persist and remain applicable to the same project.

4. **Connect**

Similarly, a new digital twin configuration can be established for an entirely new project but should only be considered if the existing configuration does not align with the specific requirements of the current project. Designing a new configuration means changing the enabling technologies being used and customizing its functionalities to define its intended purpose. For example, the digital twin configuration for the current project is only designed to generate insights from real-time data, but the new project requires predictive maintenance to save costs on operations.

Consider the following:

Making changes to the current digital twin configuration may incur additional costs as continued engagements with consultants and engineers are necessary. This may entail repeating the prior steps to verify its financial and technical feasibility as both Steps 1 and 2 may be revisited to align the solution statement with the costs of deploying certain enabling technologies and the benefits that come with it.

Step 5.2 Handover of the Digital Twin Lite

Once the Digital Twin Lite has been built, validated, and verified, the project team in conjunction with the consultants and/or technology vendors will facilitate the handover process to the DMC counterpart as part of the TOR. This process is critical to ensure sustained use of the Digital Twin Lite solution for further scaling and application to a broader scope, thus enhancing overall project outcomes.

Some key considerations for this include the following:

1. **User Training and Onboarding**

It is essential to provide comprehensive user training and onboarding to ensure new end users are familiar with the features, functionalities, and best practices of the Digital Twin Lite. Support from the technology provider may be required during this phase to address any training needs and ensure smooth user adoption.

2. **Data and Ownership Transfer**

A thorough transfer of data and ownership is necessary. This includes handing over key documents, relevant data, and licenses associated with the digital twin (both software and hardware). Ensuring all these elements are comprehensively transferred will facilitate the effective use and maintenance of the technology by the DMC counterpart.

3. **Continuity of Service**

Minimizing disruptions to ongoing operations during the handover process is crucial. To accommodate this, it may be necessary to involve overlapping access periods or other measures enabled by the technology provider. This ensures that the transition is smooth and does not adversely affect ongoing operations.

Step 5.3 Funding the Scaling of Digital Twin Lite to a Full-Scale Digital Twin

Implementing a Digital Twin Lite can help various stakeholders understand the value and advantages of digital twins within their specific domains, thereby increasing their interest in financing a full-scale digital twin. Highlighting the positive qualitative and quantitative benefits, such as cost savings or increased public collaboration, will help gain buy-in to design financing models for a full-scale digital twin. While numerous financing mechanisms and structures exist, this section outlines the most commonly adopted funding and ownership models that facilitate the transition from a Digital Twin Lite to a full-scale, multisystem digital twin.

Some typical funding modalities include the following:

1. **Grants**

Grants are often the most preferred type of financing as they do not require repayment. However, these are typically awarded in smaller amounts. Grants can be sourced from various entities, including international organizations, government bodies, and private foundations.

2. **Conventional Loans**

For larger-scale projects, governments can secure conventional loans. These loans often come with favorable terms, including low interest rates and the possibility of co-payment arrangements. Conventional loans are suitable for substantial infrastructure projects, such as the national-level 3D cadastral maps project, which has a budget allocation of $200 million with a **$40** million loan component.

3. **Outcome-Linked Loans**

Outcome-linked loans are increasingly popular, particularly for projects with specific environmental, social, and governance (ESG) targets. These loans are tied to achieving predefined outcomes, such as energy efficiency improvements or enhanced spatial data usage. This modality aligns financial incentives with project success, encouraging continuous performance improvements (Figure 15).

Figure 15: Inverse Relationship of Funding and Ownership of Digital Twins

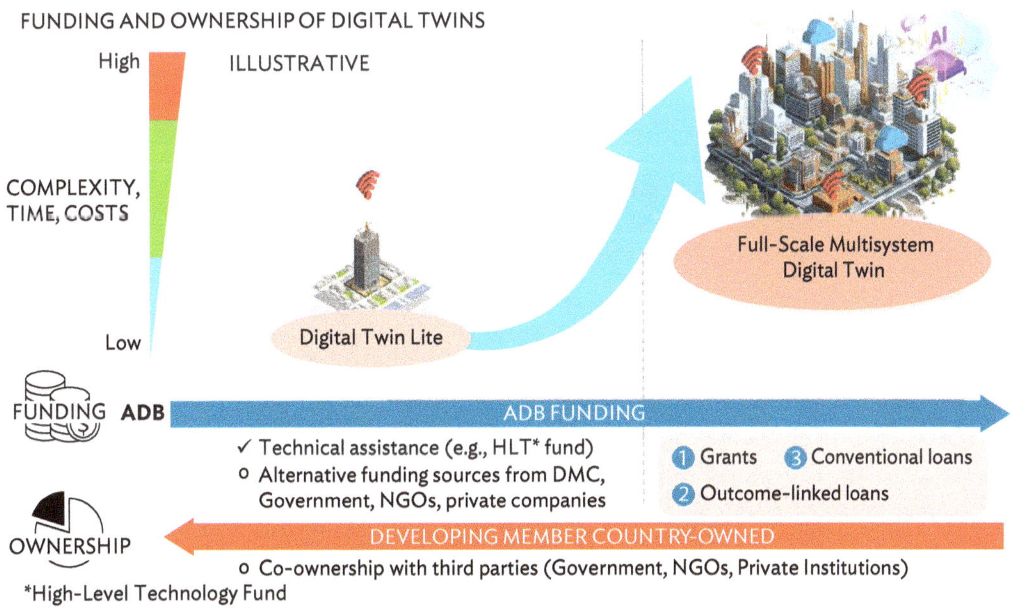

DMC = developing member country, HLT = high-level technology, NGO = nongovernment organization.

Source: Adapted from ADB and other financial institutions' technology and sustainability investment processes.

Step 5.4 How Can ADB Help Developing Member Countries Scale the Digital Twin Lite?

Even after the handover, ADB can foster continuing relations with the DMC counterpart through technical assistance and financing, and provision of data services. This section outlines the key support areas and provides practical examples of ADB's involvement.

1. **Technical Assistance and Additional Financing**

ADB operates a multi-donor trust fund known as the High-Level Technology Fund, which offers grants to promote the widespread adoption of innovative solutions in DMCs. This technical assistance and financial support can significantly aid in the development and scaling of Digital Twin Lite projects. An example of a Digital Twin Lite project that was procured through technical assistance is the Sovereign Project No. 54112-001 "Regional: Digital Twin Capabilities in Project Management."

2. **Digital Twin Data Services**

ADB can provide specialized data services that support the DMC counterpart in scaling their Digital Twin Lite. This includes integrating geospatial data and building information modeling (BIM) data through application programming interface,[4] facilitating more comprehensive and effective use of digital twin technology. The Spatial Data Analysis Explorer (SPADE) was developed as a web-based, open-source platform for centralized cloud-based server containing geospatial data, aiding in the effective analysis and integration of spatial data. In addition to being a useful tool, SPADE provides continuity benefits by enabling the reapplication of this technology, thereby enhancing engagement with DMCs. For more information, see Appendix 11.

3. **Regional Integration Support**

ADB supports the strengthening of regional cooperation and integration among DMCs to address common economic, social, and technological challenges. This regional integration can enhance the scalability and effectiveness of digital twin solutions across multiple countries. For instance, the initiative "Building Greener, Resilient Transport Infrastructure: Innovating with Artificial Intelligence and Digital Twins in Road Design in Uzbekistan" highlights how DMCs can be supported by ADB's regional integration efforts in developing robust road networks by leveraging digital twin technologies such as drone-based surveys and cloud-based data processing solutions from Skycatch.

[4] Application programming interface (API) is a set of rules that allows software applications to communicate with each other. APIs are used to exchange data, features, and functionality

Appendix 1
Key Challenges and Misconceptions About Digital Twins

As with any emerging technology, the adoption and scalability of digital twins comes with several challenges, risks, and limitations. Some of these are discussed in greater detail below, but developers of digital twin initiatives should anticipate and address how such challenges in relation to data and information, technical and human capacity, and ethical considerations should be managed to ensure a successful outcome.

1.1 Challenges in Understanding and Value Perception

Perhaps the most predominant challenge for digital twins is the lack of general understanding of what it is and the perception of the value it provides. Given that digital twins and enabling technologies are still undergoing rapid development and its deployment may be nascent in developing member countries (DMCs), it is important to not rely on a single technology or technical perspective to avoid forming a one-sided understanding of digital twins. For example, paying too much attention to 3D modeling and the visualization components, while overlooking the equally or even more important simulation extrapolation and virtual-real interaction capability available through digital twin technologies, could lead to an unbalanced development of the technology.

It is important to understand that digital twins are not a "silver bullet" and may not always be appropriate—especially if the value proposition is unclear. For instance, if developers and owners focus too much on the fine reproduction of the infrastructure asset details through high-precision technology but lack in-depth analysis of the application requirements and goals, then a digital twin may be reduced to a flashy but useless ornament. In many cases, certain enabling technologies may be sufficient to arrive at the desired value proposition rather than a digital twin. Before making any investment decision, it is important for digital twin project developers and owners to (i) develop a foundational understanding of the technology, (ii) form a problem statement to arrive at the desired value proposition, (iii) assess the cost–benefit trade-off of developing and implementing a digital twin, and (iv) discover how to get started on the digital twin road map (refer to Section 3 for more details).

1.2 Challenges in Interoperability

Abundance of data and information is a key defining characteristic of a digital twin. However, unlocking the potential value of digital twins depends on not just the quantity and quality of data, but rather enabling the interoperability of data models and standards for structuring data across sectors and the built environment, and even among different digital twins.

At the core of this challenge is the fact that field data does not follow a single, unified standard. Currently, in practice, the development of digital twins relies on multiple data sources, solutions from various developers, and has poor system interoperability. For example, data used during BIM from one technology vendor may not be easy to import to a designated digital twin platform by another technology vendor if the data is incompatible, or if the existing data is recorded as a paper-based document. This lack of a global unified consensus on digital twins' technical architecture or data accession standards makes the integration and processing of varied data difficult, leading to several drawbacks such as low data quality and insufficient data for effective decision-making.

Consequently, establishing a digital twin today requires aggregating data from multiple sources and transforming data to meet specific data format requirements—often an expensive and time-consuming exercise given the increasing volume, variety, and timescale of data. Although this can often be achieved through platforms or service that offer data normalization processes or standardized interfaces via application programming interface (API) integration, even transmitting large volumes of data may prove to be difficult for several countries, such as smaller Micronesian islands, which lack the appropriate information and communication technology (ICT) infrastructure for digitalization.

On a positive note, however, several stakeholders—from national authorities to global standards development organizations (SDOs)—have proposed the development of a standardized framework for the development and networking of digital twins. For instance, the government-mandated National Digital Twin program of the United Kingdom has created standards, guidance, and processes to enable ecosystems of multi sector digital twins, while ISO 23247 (digital twin manufacturing framework) sets a standard for applying digital twins in the manufacturing sector. While the development of such standards will provide further clarity, it will require more time and multi-stakeholder, cross-sector, and interdisciplinary consultations.

1.3 Challenges in Cybersecurity

There is an inherent data dependency between the digital twin and its physical counterpart that needs to be carefully managed as it creates vulnerabilities to data tampering and cyberattacks— such as reconnaissance, data injection attacks, data delay attacks, model corruption, and intellectual property leakage and user data breach (txOne Networks 2023). Technology experts and security leaders say digital twins can be as vulnerable to existing threats as conventional IT and operational technology (OT) environments (Pratt 2023).

> ***"Security has got to be baked right into the core of the Digital Twin you're building. It has to be there right from the onset to protect it."***
>
> **David Shaw**
> CEO of Intuitus,
> a cybersecurity firm and cochair of the Security & Trustworthiness working group at the Digital Twin Consortium

Cybersecurity threats can compromise the integrity and availability of the digital twin.

- **Threats to data integrity.** The accuracy and reliability of a digital twin depends on its data integrity—the accuracy, completeness, and quality of data as it is maintained over time. Threats to a dataset's integrity can include human error, inconsistent data formats, data collection errors, and can be compromised in case of security breach. Any manipulation or corruption of datasets pertaining to the physical infrastructure can lead to incorrect data modeling and analysis, leading to faulty decisions. Cyberattacks, such as Man-in-the-Middle attacks or data tampering, pose a significant threat to digital twins.
- **Threats to system availability.** Some cyberattacks, such as malware and ransomware, could disrupt the functionality of the digital twin, and in some cases lead to a shutdown of the physical system. Given the crucial role of IT in the transmission and processing of datasets used by digital twin, any compromise in the IT systems—ranging from network vulnerabilities, weak access controls, to outdated systems—can all have detrimental impact on the operation and reliability of the digital twin.

- **IT and OT threats.** The security of both IT and OT systems are key to a digital twin. IT systems handle the transmission, storage, and processing of data, ensuring that the digital twin has access to the latest data from its physical counterpart. On the other hand, OT systems is the hardware and software that monitors and controls devices, processes, and infrastructure. In the context of digital twins, OT systems connect Internet of Things (IoT) devices that collect data from the physical asset, and the control systems that can adjust the operation of the asset based on insights from the digital twin.

Protecting the digital twin and the interconnected IT and OT systems against such threats requires the establishment of a robust risk management process, adopting standardized framework, and upskilling project teams.

1.4 Challenges in Data Privacy and Legal Issues

In addition to and closely related to cybersecurity, many experts are also concerned about data privacy and other related legal issues on data governance, rights, and ownership.

Having data storage and processing for digital twins highly concentrated in centralized institutions can lead to an increased risk of privacy leakage and data security being compromised. Often, data sources and analyses involve the use of citizens' private data, which can easily lead to personal privacy abuse if the data cannot be effectively anonymized or placed under strict control by qualified authorities (World Economic Forum 2022). Also, there may be additional complexities in situations where there are multiple authorities contributing data to a jointly owned digital twin and the rights of the joint owners may not be clear (Fenwick Elliott n.d.). Lastly, in many instances, collecting personal data from different authorities, such as mobile devices and telecommunication service providers, satellite imagery, and other IoT devices, may be challenging or even restricted by certain DMCs, which impedes the quality and quantity of data.

Data privacy protection involves appropriate legal documentation and security compliance—such as nondisclosure agreements, project-wide confidentiality agreements, or clear data governance policies detailing data ownership—and access controls may be used to help reassure the relevant stakeholders. Role-based access can also ensure that individuals only have access to data required for their specific roles. However, from the perspective of the business and engineer teams, adding in too many security controls could hamper digital twin performance (Pratt 2023). Organizations should deploy privacy measures to avoid facing legal and financial repercussions. These issues on privacy, transparency, and accountability can also be potentially addressed through encryption or even using immutable blockchain technology to improve traceability, and to simultaneously provide a tamper-proof record of actions encouraging accountability throughout the life cycle of the project.

Digital twin developers and owners should also consider other legal issues, such as the following:

- **Intellectual property rights.** Developers and owners of the digital twin should ensure that they have adequate rights to use any third-party intellectual property and/or are protecting their own intellectual property rights in case the digital twin develops a novel approach to solving a problem.
- **Data use rights.** Developers and owners of the digital twin should ensure that they have authority from the owners of its data inputs to use it in the digital twin. This can be particularly important when using open-source data, which may be subject to data usage limitations.
- **Liability.** As with any technology solution, digital twin owners should consider what happens in case the digital twin or its related enabling technologies do not work as intended. Liability insurance, performance bonds, and/or adequate protection from technology providers should be considered by owners to protect them against any potential adverse impact, losses, and/or damages due to a decision made using the digital twin.

1.5 Challenges in Human Resources and Capacity

As in most advanced technologies, the design, plan, deployment, operations, maintenance, and monitoring of a digital twin requires integrating experts and teams from multiple disciplines such as urban management, impact analysis, demand analysis, digital technology, and algorithm modeling, to name a few.

Given the wide range of enabling technologies that underpin digital twins, and their expansive array of use-cases driven by different sector requirements, the application and implementation of digital twins can be proven difficult (MRINETWORK 2023). Stakeholders, be they ADB project officers or DMC's implementing agencies, are commonly faced with challenges relating to internal project management with regards to the technical capacity for operating and deploying digital twins. Interviews with key ADB stakeholders confirmed that DMCs that lack the enabling infrastructure for digital transformation and technology adoption tend to face this challenge.

At present, the digital twin ecosystem is dominated by experts in IT, mapping, and other professional practitioners, which requires an interdisciplinary team that possesses both business skills and technical skills. In this regard, the Centre for Digital Built Britain has put forward a Skills and Competency Framework to help infrastructure asset owners and operators and other industry professionals assess and acquire the business and technical skills needed to develop and implement a digital twin.

This challenge is commonly addressed during the preliminary stages of digital twin implementations. Identifying gaps and opportunities also involves facilitating capacity-building workshops and trainings to upskill personnel, equipping them with the knowledge and tools to operate digital twins. This shift in capacity necessitates, in addition to technical proficiency, a cultural shift within organizations through a strategic approach to change management to further increase buy-in. Embracing the transformative potential of not only digital twins, but also any digital technology needs a mindset shift in which teams recognize and capitalize on the capabilities of said technologies.

1.6 Challenges in Ethics

The integration of artificial intelligence (AI) and digital twins raises concerns around the "black box" problem. The inability to interpret how deep learning systems make their decisions due to losing track of the inputs informing those decisions, known as the "black box" problem, makes it difficult to fix the system when it produces unwanted outcomes (Blouin 2023). The lack of transparency and issue extends to digital twins and can be a cause for ethical concern if a digital twin is used as a safety measure that could have an impact on individuals' lives or well-being. Potential risk mitigations being discussed include digital twins utilizing an explainable model and/or explanation interfaces that can help us understand the rationale for decisions, safety and security safeguards, and best practices (Synengco n.d.). For instance, legal action was taken to create new safety and security standards and improve the transparency of AI through an executive order by United States President Joe Biden in October 2023 (Field and Feiner 2023).

There are also ethical concerns related to data privacy and use rights. Digital twins, if misused, have the potential to be used for the surveillance of consumption and other behaviors of citizens, leading to an invasion of privacy. For instance, a digital twin may be used to create a social scoring of citizens, which can imply discrimination and using that to target certain groups, undermining their freedom rights especially if that involves behavioral manipulation (Helbing and Sánchez-Vaquerizo 2022). This capacity for data collection makes conceivable the scenario whereby the social or medical status of people can be collected and create a new kind of discrimination by using it to determine their access rights to services, care, jobs, or facilities. Specifically in the case of health care, digital twin technology could exacerbate health disparity between the developed world and the other regions that lack the same level of technological advancement (Lal et al. 2022). This becomes more so if these datasets are used within analytics or to train machine learning/AI models, as inherent biases in the data can be further exacerbated by the model. Trustworthiness as a result of these issues can be improved by actively addressing bias through wider and diverse datasets, continuous monitoring, and interpretable or explainable models and algorithms that are fairness-aware.

1.7 Other Common Misconceptions About Digital Twins

In addition to the misconceptions discussed in Section 2.3, several other prevalent misunderstandings about digital twins persist.

Digital twinning is a relatively new concept.

The first misconception is that digital twins are a recent development. Although the terminology got coined much later, digital twins have been used in practice since the 1960s in the aerospace sector where an early iteration, and the first of its kind, was created by the National Aeronautics and Space Administration (NASA) to troubleshoot their Apollo 13 moon mission. Prior to Grieves, the industry used other terms such as "digital model" and "digital shadow" (Appendix 4), further exemplifying its diverse and progressive nature across different industries and use-cases.

Moreover, digital twins are fundamentally built upon data from the physical world and digital modeling principles, which have been applied in infrastructure development for several decades now.

Digital twins are a must-have solution for infrastructure development.

Digital twins are not a necessity in infrastructure, but their implementation can generate tremendous value at any stage, especially as countries continue to move toward digitalizing their data, such as a National Spatial Data Infrastructure. More and more systems are being implemented, which could beneficially interact with a digital twin. Leveraging this by resolving the cyber–physical interoperability and smart project design could significantly amplify the associated value of a digital twin and further "future proof" infrastructure.

Digital twins are an enterprise-level solution.

Digital twins tend to be perceived as a technologically complex solution and are only implemented on a large-scale operation. This is a widely misunderstood perception as digital twins are customizable and can be tailored to meet the specific needs of a user down to an individual process or asset component. They can be introduced as a budget-friendly, entry-level solution for smaller operations, and can be adapted as the operations expand to a larger scale.

Digital twin is just a visual model of the physical asset.

Since digital twins are able to integrate data from various sources, their capabilities can range from visualizing static (historical) data to real-time dynamic data. Digital twins have the potential to evolve beyond two-dimensional (2D) and/or three-dimensional (3D) visualization and can expand with the addition of more technological building blocks.

Appendix 2
Use-Case Library

The analyzed digital twin applications are listed in the use-case library (see provided link), organized into primary sectors and indicative maturity levels. Details and further analysis, including key enabling technologies used and value-add benefits realized, can be found in this full database.

2.1 Water and Urban Development

With over 50% of Asia and the Pacific's population living in cities, the region's rapid and often erratic urbanization has resulted in growing deficits in infrastructure investments to make cities more livable (ADB 2023c). Some 600 million people in urban areas and 1.5 billion people living in rural environments still lack adequate water supply. ADB's priorities to help resolve these issues indicate support toward building digital technology capacity and innovation. The project, Mainstreaming Water Resilience in Asia and the Pacific, facilitates the use of digital and remote sensing technologies, providing an enabling platform for applying digital twins (ADB 2023d).

Water and urban development is the top sector where digital twins see the most applications worldwide, commonly at a Level 2 maturity. Within Asia and the Pacific, digital twins within the sector also see the highest concentration, reaching around 40% of the aggregated success stories. Digital twins, which serve to make such investments more efficient, are heavily concentrated around smart city initiatives both globally and regionally. The common use-cases in the sector are summarized in Table A2.1.

Table A2.1: Overview of Common Use-Cases in Water and Urban Development

Use-Cases	Application Details
Visualization or analytics to aid urban planning	• Aurecon – Melbourne Quarter (Level 1) • University of Bradford – Virtual Bradford (Level 2) • Tekuchi – London Digital Twin (Level 2) • Dassault – Digital Twin: Singapore Smart City (Level 2) • The Digital Twin of Zurich for urban planning (Level 2) • ADB Project – Penang Smart Mobility (Level 3) • Bentley – Singapore Land Authority, Country Scale Digital Twin (Level 4)
Optimization of design before construction	• AVEVA – Harnessing digital twin technology benefits for new water plant designs (Level 2) • Softengi – 3D Building Model: Ciegno Case (Level 3) • Project Controls Cubed LLC & Bentley – Echowater Project (Level 3) • Bentley – Geoinfo Services, access to clean drinking water (Level 3) • Mott Macdonald – Kidston pumped hydro station (Level 4)
Construction life cycle and process management	• Sensat – Canada Water Masterplan (Level 2) • Dassault – POSCO A&C construction virtual twin (Level 2) • Leica – In slab risk mitigation: A case for 3D laser scanning in commercial construction (Level 2) • Bentley – Siemensstadt Square (Level 3)

Use-Cases	Application Details
Monitoring and inspection for maintenance and risk prevention	• E8ight – How simulation can help prevent disasters (Level 2) • Bentley – St. Peter's Basilica (Level 3) • Siemens – Water's App: SIWA LeakPlus (Level 3) • Bentley – Yuba Water Agency automates monitoring of California's second tallest dam (Level 3)
Integrated facility or asset management	• Aurecon – University of Melbourne (WEBS) (Level 2) • Mott Macdonald – Five Fords Treatment Plant (Level 2) • Autodesk – Toronto Office, Canada (Level 4) • Arup – Neuron Digital, One Taikoo Place (Level 5)

Sources: Use-cases were sourced from the respective technology vendors or relevant publications.

With the nature of this sector, digital twin uses are focused on managing and assisting entire assets and systems. Consequently, use-cases in this sector are primarily for visualizing and analyzing large assets and their geospatial surroundings. In doing so, not only do digital twins allow benefits visualization and monitoring within water and urban development, but they also provide improvements in productivity (efficiency), operations and maintenance (O&M), and decision-making.

UNIVERSITY OF MELBOURNE (WEBS)

Integrated asset management | **Australia**

WATER & URBAN DEV.

Level 2

The primary objective is the development of a user-friendly 'as-built' model for the recently completed bioscience faculty. To achieve this goal, an interactive and real-time digital twin will be implemented to seamlessly support asset management integration ensuring greater efficiency in terms of operations.

This initiative surpasses conventional static models by leveraging advanced technology, providing users with an engaging and dynamic real-time experience when interacting with the facility. The implementation of a virtual twin in this scenario not only improves the overall asset management but also establishes a standard for sustainable, user-friendly practices for infrastructure development for universities.

The digital twin will also provide valuable data for the decision-making and experience of university leadership, researchers, and students, while enabling proactive crisis management during events like the coronavirus disease (COVID-19) pandemic.

Technology provider: Aurecon, through Dashboarding Engagement Hubs
Time period: N/A
Other information: Includes dashboarding, interactive elements, point cloud mapping, and conversion to information models

Key enabling technologies

- ● Data Modeling and Visualization
- ● ICT / IoT
- ○ Artificial Intelligence (AI)/ Machine Learning
- ● Spatial Computing (CAD, GIS, GPS, GNSS)
- ○ Cloud Computing
- ● Software and Platforms
- ○ Security
- ○ Others

Key benefits from digital twin

- ● Visualization and monitoring
- ● Informed decision-making
- ○ Resource optimization and loss reduction
- ○ Productivity gains
- ● Improve operations, inspection, maintenance
- ○ Improve or optimize financial performance
- ○ Improve quality
- ○ Increase customer satisfaction
- ● Improved knowledge and collaboration
- ○ Security and safety
- ○ Predictive intelligence
- ● Risk management and resilience
- ○ Improved environmental sustainability
- ○ Others

Sources: University of Melbourne, Aurecon. Images reproduced with permission from Aurecon.

2.2 Transport

Transport, essentially functioning as the world's circulatory system by enabling the mobility of people and products to be interconnected globally, remains a prime avenue for reorienting capital for both climate risk and resilience. This sector takes up more than 30% of Asia and the Pacific's required climate-adjusted investment by 2030 to maintain growth and effectively address climate change (ADB 2023e).

Globally, the transport sector ranks second in terms of available applications of digital twins, with Level 2 maturity use-cases as the most common. Global precedents see a concentration of digital twin uses in the road and aviation subsectors, followed by rail and maritime. The common use-cases in this sector are summarized in Table A2.2.

Table A2.2: Overview of Common Use-Cases in Transport

Use-Case	Example of Applications
Virtual training and capacity building	Aurecon – Redfern station signal sighting (Level 2) Beamo – Japanese airline digitizing its training (Level 2)
Optimizing design and construction of an asset	Aurecon – Smart Stations (Level 1) Dassault – Digital twin for railway design - China Railway Design Corporation (Level 2) National Underground Asset Register (NUAR) Pilot Programme (Level 2) Dassault – MerConcept (Level 2) Bentley – Parkdale Level Crossing Removal (Level 3) ADB Project – Greener, Resilient Transport Infrastructure, Uzbekistan (Level 3)
Monitoring and management of traffic, networks, routes, projects	ADB Project – Digital twin capabilities in project management, Nauru (Level 1) Spinview – MTR: Reducing travel disruption and delays (Level 2) Bentley – Johor Bahru–Singapore rapid transit systems (Level 2) Agonics & Aurecon – Australian Rail Track Corporation (Level 2) 51World – Remapping the morning commute in the PRC with digital twins (Level 3) Hypothetical Smart City with autonomous traffic management (Level 5)
Visual scanning and inspection for repair or maintenance	Spinview – Nuova Tech AB - Faster and efficient road repairs (Level 2) Akselos – Optimizing FPSO Inspection ROI (Level 2) Bentley – Robert St. Bridge - Bridge Monitoring (Level 3) SAP – Stavå, bridge in distress sends warning (Level 3) Akselos – Life extension for a ship loader (Level 4)
Disaster prediction and safety management	Bentley – I-70 Floyd Hills to veterans' memorial tunnels (Level 3) Bentley – Collins Engineers Uses Digital Inspection to Restore Iconic Pedestrian Bridge in Minneapolis (Level 3) Fujitsu and Hexagon – Digital twin tech aids predictive disaster and traffic safety management (Level 4)

Sources: Use-cases were sourced from the respective technology vendors or relevant publications.

Applications in this sector also range across the life cycle of a transport infrastructure project— from design and construction to operations. Most digital twins within the transport sector fall within replicating assets or systems rather than specific components. Throughout these multiple use-cases, organizations typically see a return on improved productivity, informed decision-making, and risk management, which all enable better security and/or safety, improved O&M, and optimum financial performance.

DIGITAL TWIN CAPABILITIES IN PROJECT MANAGEMENT

TRANSPORT

Remote monitoring | **Nauru**

Level 1

The Nauru project involved constructing and developing wharf and port infrastructure. Given the size and remoteness of Nauru, there were limitations in resources, capacity, and difficulties in monitoring the construction of the project.

The aim of implementing a digital twin was to collect and analyze valuable data for monitoring progress, recognizing potential risks and challenges, and determining suitable responses throughout construction and to appraise the medium-and long term project effects once it concludes. A drone-based platform was developed for remote project monitoring and to generate a 3D constantly updated image of the site. A drone is deployed to capture images of the site which is then incorporated into the 3D model.

Technology provider: Skycatch Inc., CSIRO Data61
Time period: 2020 – 2025
Other information: N/A

Key enabling technologies

- ● Data Modeling and Visualization
- ● ICT/IoT
- ○ Artificial Intelligence (AI)/ Machine Learning
- ● Spatial Computing (CAD, GIS, GPS, GNSS)
- ○ Cloud Computing
- ● Software and Platforms
- ○ Security
- ○ Others

Key benefits from Digital Twin

- ● Visualization and monitoring
- ● Informed decision-making
- ○ Resource optimization and loss reduction
- ○ Productivity gains
- ● Improve operations, inspection, maintenance
- ● Improve or optimize financial performance
- ○ Improve quality
- ○ Increase customer satisfaction
- ○ Improved knowledge and collaboration
- ○ Security and safety
- ○ Predictive intelligence
- ● Risk managementand resilience
- ○ Improved environmental sustainability
- ○ Others

Sources: Skycatch Inc., CSIRO Data61. Photo by ADB.

2.3 Energy

Energy, which is essential to fueling people's livelihoods and fostering comprehensive socioeconomic progress, continues to face challenges in universal access, security, and sustainability. Over 150 million people in developing Asia and the Pacific still lack access to electricity, even as the region accounts for over 50% of global carbon emissions (of which more than half originates from energy or heat). Energy and power, nevertheless, make up 56% of Asia and the Pacific's required climate-adjusted investment by 2030 (ADB 2023f).

Both globally and within Asia and the Pacific, the energy sector ranks third in terms of number of digital twin use-cases. Overall, use-cases were primarily focused on oil and gas, renewable energy, followed by other alternative energy generation and management (nuclear energy and utilities and/or energy management). The energy sector sees a common digital twin maturity levels 2–3. Common use-cases in the sector are summarized in Table A2.3.

Table A2.3: Overview of Common Use-Cases in Energy

Use-cases	Application Details
Optimizing the design and construction of a project	• Sensat – National Grid (Level 2) • Bentley – PowerChina, Xianning Chibi Substation (Level 3)
Optimize plant operations	• Bentley – SAMI, digital twin application project of electrolytic aluminum engineering (Level 3)
Management, assessment, and maintenance of plant or asset	• Unity, Zutari – Sidwawa Substation (Level 1) • Bentley – Asset management of hydropower project (Level 3) • Jungle AI – Power forecasting for wind farm maintenance scheduling optimization (Level 3) • Akselos – Digital twins for structural assessment of power stations, Ireland (Level 4)
Monitoring status of plant and surroundings	• Softengi – Computer vision software for drones in the utility sector (Level 3)
Smart grid management	• Hypothetical – European Union, Smart Grid Management (Level 5)

Sources: Use-cases were sourced from the respective technology vendors or relevant publications.

With real-time data implementation supported by cloud computing, the energy sector sees digital twins replicating assets and systems to design, operate, monitor, and maintain. A common benefit derived from digital twins in this sector, outside the three most prolific themes (productivity, decision-making, visualization and/or monitoring) is optimizing the financial performance of assets and projects.

Sidwawa Substation Power Transmission

Asset upgrade planning and development | **South Africa**

ENERGY

Level 1

Sidwawa's substation's old equipment was replaced with new equipment to increase the reliability and capacity of the substation, but the footprint of the equipment was not compatible with the legislation regarding fire risks and equipment safety.

Zutari used innovative 3D modeling of the substation that provides more detail on the spaces in the structures to aid in adjusting the layout of the equipmentto compensate for inadequate electrical clearances. The 3D images allowed for the virtual arrangement of the equipmentto figure it how to meet the standards on electrical clearances, and it mitigated and lowered risks of an oil spill.

Significant productivity gains were also made from the intelligent data links embedded in the equipment properties. Prevalent challenges when working in confined spaces and safety zones were easier to overcome with the 3D modeling.

Technology provider: Unity, Zutari
Time period: N/A
Other information: N/A

Key enabling technologies

- ● Data Modeling and Visualization
- ○ ICT / IoT
- ○ Artificial Intelligence (AI)/ Machine Learning
- ● Spatial Computing (CAD, GIS, GPS, GNSS)
- ● Cloud Computing
- ● Software and Platforms
- ○ Security
- ○ Others

Key benefits from Digital Twin

- ● Visualization and monitoring
- ● Informed decision-making
- ● Resource optimization and loss reduction
- ● Productivity gains
- ○ Improve operations, inspection, maintenance
- ○ Improve or optimize financial performance
- ● Improve quality
- ● Increase customer satisfaction
- ● Improved knowledge and collaboration
- ● Security and safety
- ○ Predictive intelligence
- ● Risk management and resilience
- ● Improved environmental sustainability
- ○ Others

Sources: Unity, Zutari. Image reproduced with permission from Zutari.

2.4 Other Sectors

Apart from infrastructure asset development in the previously mentioned three sectors, the remaining few industries also make up a fair portion of global digital twin use-cases. Of the approximately 40% of remaining applications globally, uses in the industry and trade sector are the most prominent, taking up 18% of the total use-cases worldwide. This is followed by human and social development at 7%, agriculture and related subsectors at 6%, ICT at 4%, and public sector management at 1%.

Industry and Trade

- Primary subsectors: General manufacturing (45%), industrial estates (27%)
- General trend: Showing advanced implementation of digital twins, supported by the sector's prior initiatives in Industry 4.0 (digitization of the manufacturing industry through cyber-physical systems).

Human and Social Development

- Primary subsectors: Health and well-being (63%), education (27%)
- General trend: Focused on supporting improvements in public health facilities and extending access to education and learning through technology.

Agriculture, Food, Nature, and Rural Development

- Primary subsectors: Environment and conservation (100%)
- General trend: Heavily concentrated on environmental sustainability and resilience, especially on coastal environments.

Information and Communication Technology

- Primary subsectors: Technology development (e.g., data centers, network platforms) (62%), telecommunications (38%)
- General trend: Cross-cutting through other sectors. For instance, city-scale digital twins to maximize urban 5G coverage or 5G private network smart studios within industrial parks and construction.

Public Sector Management and Governance

- Primary subsectors: Government (50%), Smart cities (37%)
- General trend: Rare applications of digital twins. There is potential to aid governments through modeling agencies to optimize information and bottlenecks in their reliance on outdated internal systems, such as legacy hardware and software, and paper-based processes.

Finance

- Primary subsectors: Private finance; banking, financial service, and insurance (BFSI) (Altair 2023).
- General trend: Rare applications of digital twins. Sources and surveys show that digital twin concepts are being implemented in fintech, allocating financial information to optimize funding, and modeling financial processes for decision-making.

These sectors see digital twins being primarily enabled through the same key technologies (modeling, visualization, Internet of Things [IoT], and others). Sectors such as agriculture have higher use of spatial computing, while finance commonly uses cloud computing technologies. Cumulatively, digital twins in these sectors will benefit informed decision-making and productivity and support the implementing agency's ability to visualize and monitor necessary elements in their operations.

The following are the most commonly seen use-cases among these sectors (Table A2.4).

Table A2.4: Overview of Common Use-Cases in Other Sectors

Use-Cases	Application Details
Industry and Trade	
Optimizing design and construction process of asset	• Bentley – MCC Capital Linyi Steel Plant (Level 3)
Optimizing manufacturing processes, operations, and maintenance	• Beamo – Smart Factories (Level 2) • Siemens – A digital twin for the milling process (Level 3)
Agriculture, Food, Nature, and Rural Development	
Geography and coastal surveying or monitoring	• Leica – Monitoring Alpine glaciers and climate change with 3D laser scanning (Level 2) • Leica – High-density airborne LiDAR sensor ideal for challenging coastal survey of Sylt (Level 3)
Planning and forecasting for natural risk mitigation	• Graffiquo – Disaster planning and mitigation - Typhoon preparedness and response (Level 2) • NVIDIA – Earth-2 (Level 3)
Smart farming and agriculture	• Leica – Tank inspections (Level 2) • Hypothetical smart farming (Level 5)
Human and Social Development	
Social asset life-cycle management (from design to operations)	• Matterport – Healthcare Trust of America (Level 1) • Fujitsu – Baptist Health (Level 2) • Aveva – New Hospital of Orleans (Level 3)
Virtual and remote education or health care	• Texas A&M – Scalable smart manufacturing workforce development (Level 2) • Dassault – University of Adelaide design solutions (Level 3) • Hypothetical autonomous health-care monitoring and patient care (Level 5)
Public Sector Management and Governance	
Mapping development to monitor progress or plan investment	• Infrastructure Mapping Application for London (Level 2)
Monitoring and forecasting to improve public safety	• Softengi – Web platform solution for natural hazards (Level 3)
Optimizing government agencies, assets, and augmenting public services	• Hypothetical government system twin (Level 2)
Finance	
Optimizing funding and allocating financial information	• Giraffe – EEC New City (Level 2) • Softengi – Machine learning-powered smart algorithms for finance (Level 3)
Analytics for advanced financial trading and economy assessment	• Hypothetical algorithmic trading (Level 5)

LiDAR = light detection and ranging.
Source: Use-cases were sourced from the respective technology vendors or relevant publications.

TANK INSPECTIONS

Handling agricultural products on a large scale necessitates the storage of vast quantities of produce in tanks and silos. The maintenance of these vessels is a significant undertaking where PT Wilmar's local project team is required to routinely examine all above ground storage tanks, providing management with measurements that assess the structures' integrity. In the past, tank inspection was a labor-intensive manual process.

PT Wilmar Indonesia sought a way to streamline the tank inspection procedure, aiming for greater speed without the need for additional manpower. The new solution had to enhance the efficiency of the process without compromising the accuracy of the data or the safety of the team. They opted to incorporate laser scanning into their operations such as Leica RTC360 laser scanners for digitally scanning the silos and employed Cyclone 3DR software for data analysis.

Specific benefits:

- Inspection time decreased from 4-5 days to 1 day
- Efficiency increased by 4,500%

Technology provider: Leica Geosystems
Time period: N/A
Other information: Utilizes Leica RTC360 laser scanners and Cyclone 3DR software

Key enabling technologies

● Data Modeling and Visualization
● ICT / IoT
○ Artificial Intelligence (AI)/ Machine Learning
○ Spatial Computing (CAD, GIS, GPS, GNSS)
○ Cloud Computing
● Software and Platforms
○ Security
○ Others

Key benefits from Digital Twin

● Visualization and monitoring
○ Informed decision-making
● Resource optimization and loss reduction
● Productivity gains
● Improve operations, inspection, maintenance
○ Improve or optimize financial performance
● Improve quality
○ Increase customer satisfaction
○ Improved knowledge and collaboration
● Security and safety
○ Predictive intelligence
○ Risk management and resilience
○ Improved environmental sustainability
○ Others

Source: Leica Geosystems.

Appendix 3

Harnessing the Power of Artificial Intelligence

Integrated into digital twins, artificial intelligence (AI) has made potential applications truly versatile across many of the key sectors. Given the rate of adoption and evolution of AI, the possibilities may go far beyond the use-cases, as discussed below.

Versatile Capabilities Enabled by Artificial Intelligence

AI enables **advanced data processing and analytics** to swiftly clean, evaluate, or even generate datasets that are fed into digital twins for deeper, more valuable insight (Akbar 2024; AWS n.d.). Beyond the sheer volume and levels of datasets and diverse computational models allowing for applications on complex, multifactorial provincial- or national-level projects, digital twins can also be used for unique applications such as anomaly detection.

AI enables **improved interactivity** through natural language interfaces or generated virtual environments to explore and navigate the digital twin (Cosmas et al. 2024). By enhancing the ease of use of otherwise complex digital twins, it could uncover previously unexplored knowledge gaps, further strengthening their capabilities.

Complex predictions are possible with AI (Akbar 2024; Panaro, Parlow, and Amman 2024) by generating multiple diverse scenarios, possibilities, and responses of the physical environment for simulation. This will be particularly valuable for future climate challenges as economics continue to exceed the limits of planetary boundaries, and the complexity of interconnected ecosystems requires equally complex predictions.

AI enables the **optimization** of processes (AWS. n.d.; Kreuzer, Papapetrou, and Zdravkovic 2024) by leveraging machine learning and training to improve the efficiency of the eventual physical twin. Allowing this fine-tuning minimizes potential costs and the use of scarce and emissive resources while maximizing sustainability and operational benefits from projects.

AI enables **adaptative decision-making** to respond to changing conditions of assets, systems, or processes and making real-time digital twin adjustments (Panaro, Parlow, and Amman 2024). The combination of the above capabilities allows nuanced and rapid responses that are especially valuable in crisis situations.

AI enables **autonomous learning** to evolve and improve performance through interactions with data, needing little to no human intervention (Bhoda 2024). Ethical safeguards and other preventive measures must be in place, however, in anan optimal scenario, applications of autonomous learning could prevent implicit biases or misjudgment, and genuinely foster an equitable and fair society.

As organizations harness AI for predictive analytics and real-time decision-making, they increasingly rely on digital twins to create virtual replicas, underscoring a new era of data-driven innovation.

The success and versatility of AI for digital twins are self-evident, as the adoption rate of digital twin exhibits a strong correlation with the growth of AI. As Figure A3 shows, the proliferation of digital twins has surged since the first "widespread" generative illustration model "DALL-E," and it is expected to continue to grow significantly until 2030.

Figure A3: Symbiotic Evolution of Digital Twins and Artificial Intelligence

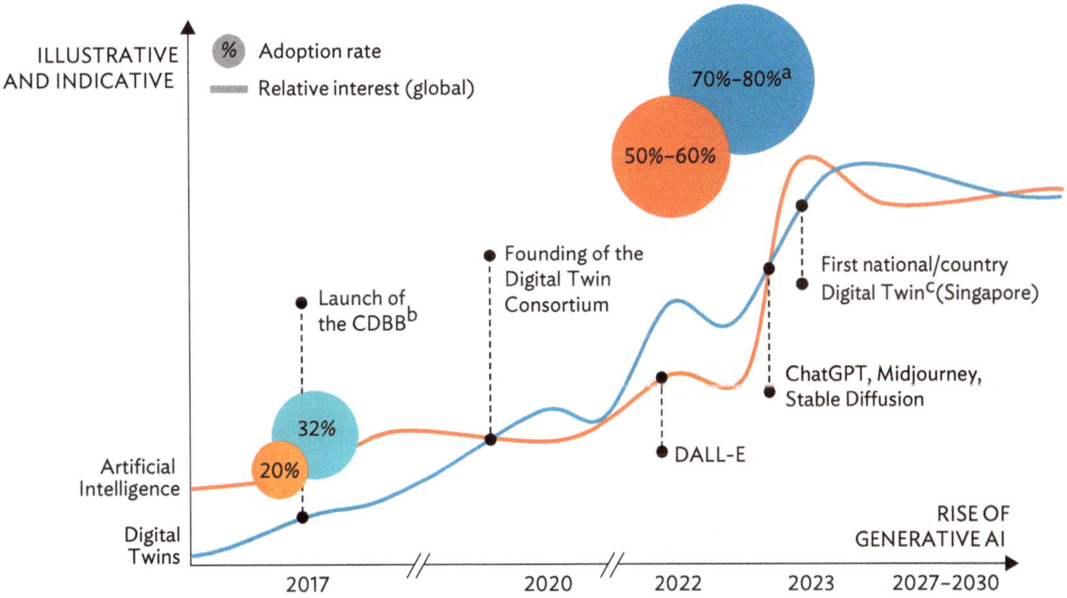

AI = artificial intelligence.

[a] Estimated based on various sources.

[b] Centre for Digital Built Britain.

[c] A. Walker. 2023. Singapore's Digital Twin – From Science Fiction to Hi-Tech Reality.

Source: Author. Data sourced from Google trends, IBM, Altair, Gartner, McKinsey, Deloitte, Gitnux, IOT Analytics, and other market research sources.

This symbiotic relationship has fueled significant parallel market growth, with the global AI market expected to surge from its current size of $200 billion in 2023 to $300 billion–$400 billion in 2027, and the digital twin market from $16 billion in 2023 to $74 billion in 2027.

Appendix 4
Other Classifications of Digital Twins

Understanding the various classifications play a vital role in assessing whether digital twins are appropriate for the project or not. These will suggest the multiple angles of consideration for each specific use-case.

Classification Based on Subtypes

During 2016–2018, Michael Grieves, chief scientist of the Digital Twin Institute, together with John Vickers of the National Aeronautics and Space Administration (NASA), finally coined the term "digital twin." Together, they suggested that digital twins should be divided into three subtypes:

- **Digital Twin Prototype (DTP).** A DTP is undertaken before the physical asset is built (TWI, n.d.). It serves as the prototype of a physical asset containing all relevant information of the physical attributes (properties, designs, parameters, and others), making it a vital part of its life cycle (Grunitz 2023; Fenstermaker 2022).
- **Digital Twin Instance (DTI).** A DTI, created from the DTP, is the twin of a physical asset through its life cycle (Raghunathan 2019). Although the DTI starts with baseline information from its prototype, the DTI improves over the asset's life cycle as it gathers more operational data through various inputs (e.g., sensors, asset and warranty information, service records, and others) (Fenstermaker 2022).
- **Digital Twin Aggregate (DTA).** A DTA is an aggregate of many DTIs (Raghunathan 2019), combining data and information from multiple DTIs for learning, interrogation, and running prognostics (TWI, n.d.; Grunitz, 2023). DTAs enable the simulation and understanding of group behavior rather than individual behavior (e.g., all the wind turbines in a wind farm rather than just one wind turbine) (Fenstermaker 2022).

Classification Based on Data Integration and Exchange

During 2018, researchers from Fraunhofer Austria Research GmbH differentiated digital twins based on their level of integration of the technology and data exchange with the real world, which are as follows (Kritzinger et al. 2018):

- **Digital Model (DM).** The DM does not automate the data exchanges between the physical and the digital model. All the data flows are done manually, and no change in the state of the physical or digital model has direct consequences to the other.
- **Digital Shadow (DS).** What sets it apart from the DM is that the DS has an automatic, unidirectional flow of data from the physical to the digital shadow. Internet of Things (IoT) devices and sensors are used to automatically collect and feed data into the virtual system. A change in the physical object can interfere with the digital, but the opposite does not occur.
- **Digital Twin (DT).** An automatic, bidirectional flow of data links the physical and the digital assets. Like the DS, the physical can control the digital, but in this case, the digital also interferes with the physical. This constant flow, which is fully integrated, is what makes a digital twin. Further, advanced forms may integrate artificial intelligence (AI) to automate even solutions or actions (Figure A4.1).

Figure A4.1: Data Flows for a Digital Model, Digital Shadow, and Digital Twin

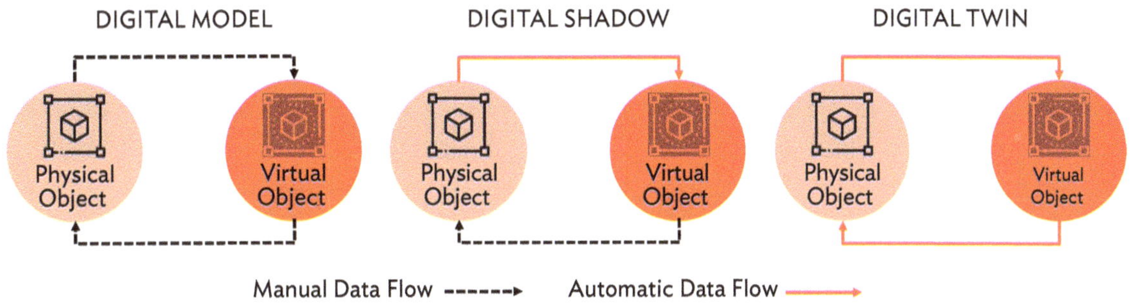

Source: A. Andrade. 2022. *The 4 Levels of the Digital Twin Technology–2023.* Vidya.

Classification Based on Scale of Coverage and Application

Various technology corporations, such as IBM, have classified and distinguished digital twins based on their level of magnification and area of application (Figure A4.2). The following four main digital twin types are proposed:

- **Component Twin.** This is the smallest scale of digital twin implementation, which is a virtual representation of a well-defined, individual part of a product, asset, or system. However, it does not mean that a Component Twin is the smallest part of the physical object. Component Twins are particularly valuable in mirroring integral parts that have a direct impact on the overall performance and functionality of the asset.
- **Asset Twin.** This next classification of digital twin implementation is a virtual representation of a product or asset. It comprises two or more Component Twins, describing how individual components of an asset interact and operate together on a wider scale to perform certain tasks. For instance, although the pitch bearing is a critical wind turbine component, its performance cannot be viewed in isolation without understanding its interactions with the companion components.
- **System Twin.** Further up the scale of digital twin implementation is the System Twin (sometimes referred to as a Unit Twin), which can be classified as a combination of individual Asset Twins to describe how an entire system operates. This scale of implementation allows users to observe the interaction between assets, and how they work together to form a fully functional system.
- **Process Twin.** The Process Twin further enhances the function of the previous digital twin classification by going beyond a single system to encompass the entire operational environment. Process Twins combine multiple systems to create a complex set of workflows, allowing users to track the performance and level of coordination between all assets and individual components. Since the focus of the Process Twin is the linkages between systems, oftentimes, the Component or Asset Twin can be developed afterward.

Figure A4.2: Range of Applicability of Digital Twins

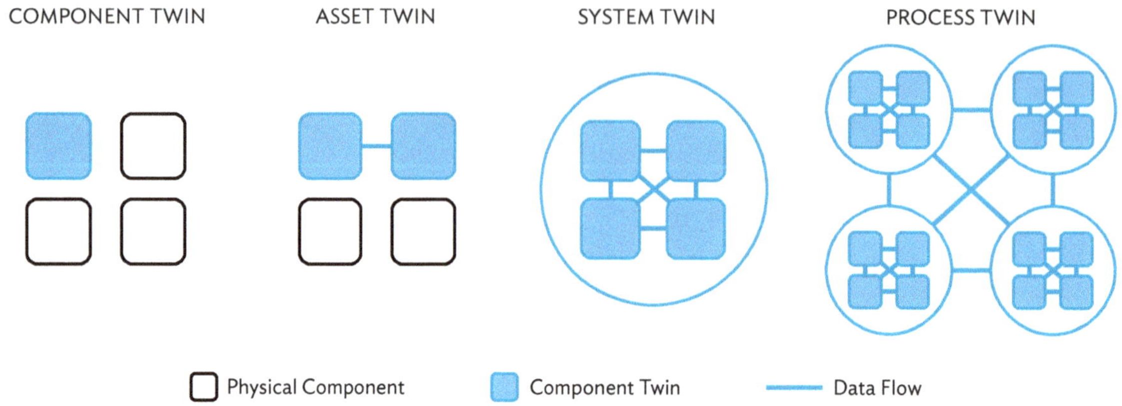

Source: Adapted from Z. Liu et al. 2023. *Digital Twin for Predictive Maintenance.* doi:10.1117/12.2660270.

Classification Based on a Three-Dimensional Matrix

Through the use of a three-dimensional matrix, this classification takes a more minute approach to determining the type of digital twin. In its 2023 report, IoT Analytics[1] refined their cuboid featuring three primary dimensions, representing a total of 210 different potential combinations of what a digital twin can mirror and can do, and at which point in time, as discussed below:

- **Life-cycle phases.** Represented in the X-axis, this dimension is reflective of the project life-cycle stage(s) at which the digital twin is being deployed, the *Design, Build, Operate, Maintain, Optimize, and Decommission* phases.
- **Hierarchical levels.** Represented in the Y-axis, this dimension closely resembles the previous classification of digital twins based on level of magnification and area of application. These hierarchical levels increase in complexity from *Information Twins, Component Twins, Product Twins (Asset), System Twins, to Multi-system Twins (Process).* An Information Twin is described as a digital representation of any information that does not make up a part or component of a physical object, such as instruction manuals or procedures presented in digital format. With the new update to the report, IoT Analytics no longer considers an Information Twin as the most basic hierarchical level of a digital twin.
- **Most common uses.** This final dimension, as represented in the Z-axis, reflects the seven most common uses of digital twins. Also listed in the order of complexity and required computing power are to *Digitize, Visualize, Simulate, Emulate, Extract, Orchestrate,* and *Predict.* The matrix classification acknowledges that uses will invariably range in specificity and breadth in this dimension through additional "Nth" uses that cannot be compartmentalized into these seven categories (refer to Appendix 2 for further uses).

This classification approach reflects the flexibility inherent in the nature of the digital twin concept (Figure A4.3). This approach further demonstrates the increasing complexity of digital twins as additional dimensions are brought into consideration. Exemplified by the "Digital-Twin 8-Dimension Model," the possible combinations could reach up to 10,000 (Kim et al. 2023). Rather than asking *"What type of digital twin?,"* a multidimensional matrix demonstrates that it is more valuable to instead ask *"A digital twin to do what in what context?"*

[1] IoT Analytics is a Germany-based global provider of market insights and business intelligence across the tech stack, and is focused on IoT, AI, Cloud, Edge, and Industry 4.0.

Figure A4.3: An Application Example of the Matrix Classification

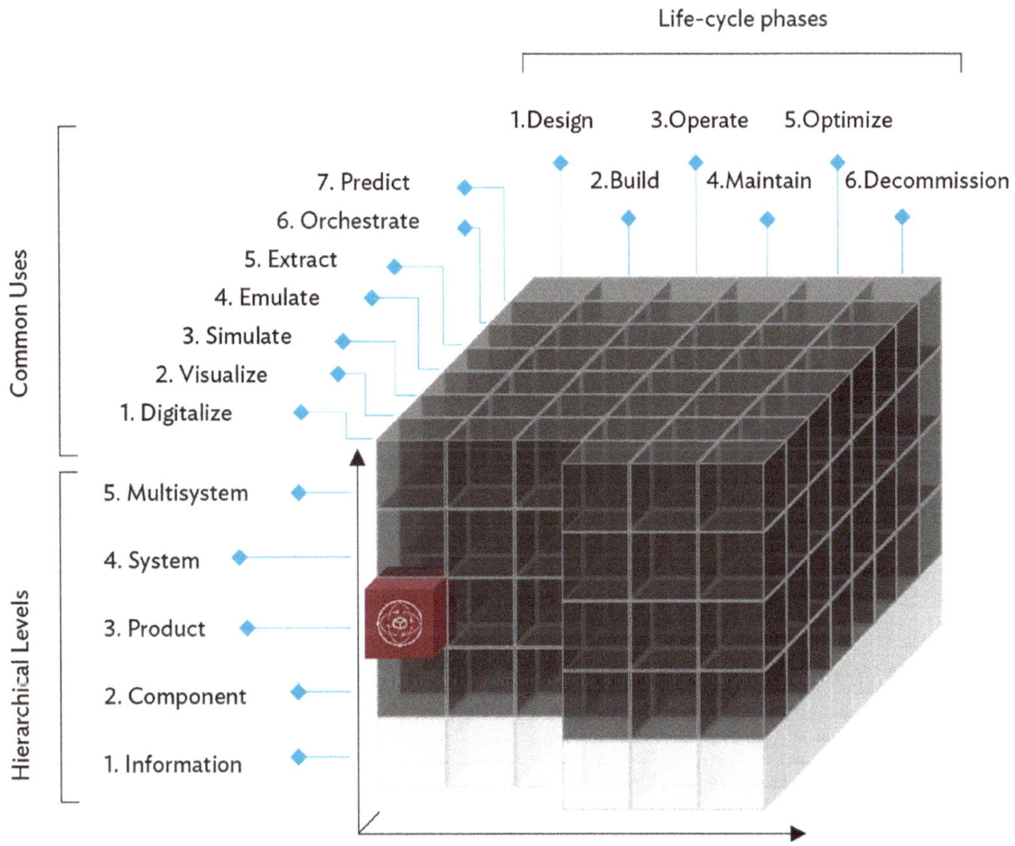

Source: Adapted from the IOT Analytics' digital twin matrix classification.

Appendix 5

Range and Complexities of Digital Twins

The key advantages of digital twins are their flexibility and dynamism. The configuration of different enabling technologies opens up a myriad of application possibilities that generate different values for the implementing party. At the very basic level, organizations can selectively gather and observe data that hold intrinsic value, such as observing traffic levels at a specific intersection, analyzing wear and tear of certain support pillars of a bridge, or monitoring water flow through an asset's piping system. Valuable use cases can be found at any point throughout a project's life cycle. As such, diagnosing gaps where the digital twin can bring the most value is paramount for the implementing organization.

Through a combination of stakeholder interviews and desktop research, over 200 unique digital twin application examples were identified and combined into the Digital Twin Use-Case Library. In analyzing these use-cases, it was found that four out of 10 digital twin use-cases were in the water and urban development sector, with smart city initiatives being the most common trend (Figure A5.1). Although around 50% of these applications were from projects located in Europe, Asia and the Pacific came a close second.

Figure A5.1: Sector Breakdown of Digital Twin Applications

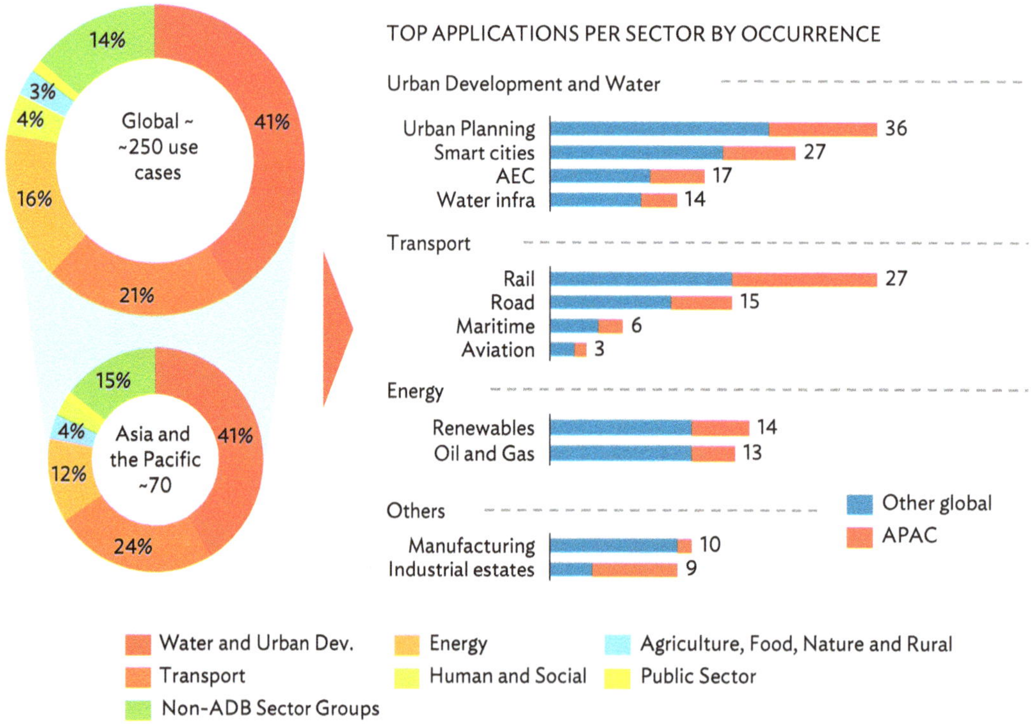

APAC = Asia and the Pacific, ADB = Asian Development Bank, AEC = ASEAN Economic Community..
Source: Author. Based on author's analysis of a compilation of over 200 publicly available use-cases.

A further examination of the use-case library revealed the following:

- **Digital twins are more common in countries with high digital readiness.** Countries with high digital twin implementations show a clear correlation to high global digital readiness indices—comprising the Human Capital Index, Technology Adoption Index, and Technology Infrastructure Index (Figure A5.2). The People's Republic of China, France, Italy, the United Kingdom, and the United States ranked among the top countries to showcase digital twin success stories. Within Asia and the Pacific, digital twins were also more prominent in developed countries like Australia, the People's Republic of China, Japan, and the Republic of Korea, and in general, follow the same trend as being the top countries of the region for digital readiness.

Figure A5.2: Digital Readiness Index in Select Countries Across Asia and the Pacific

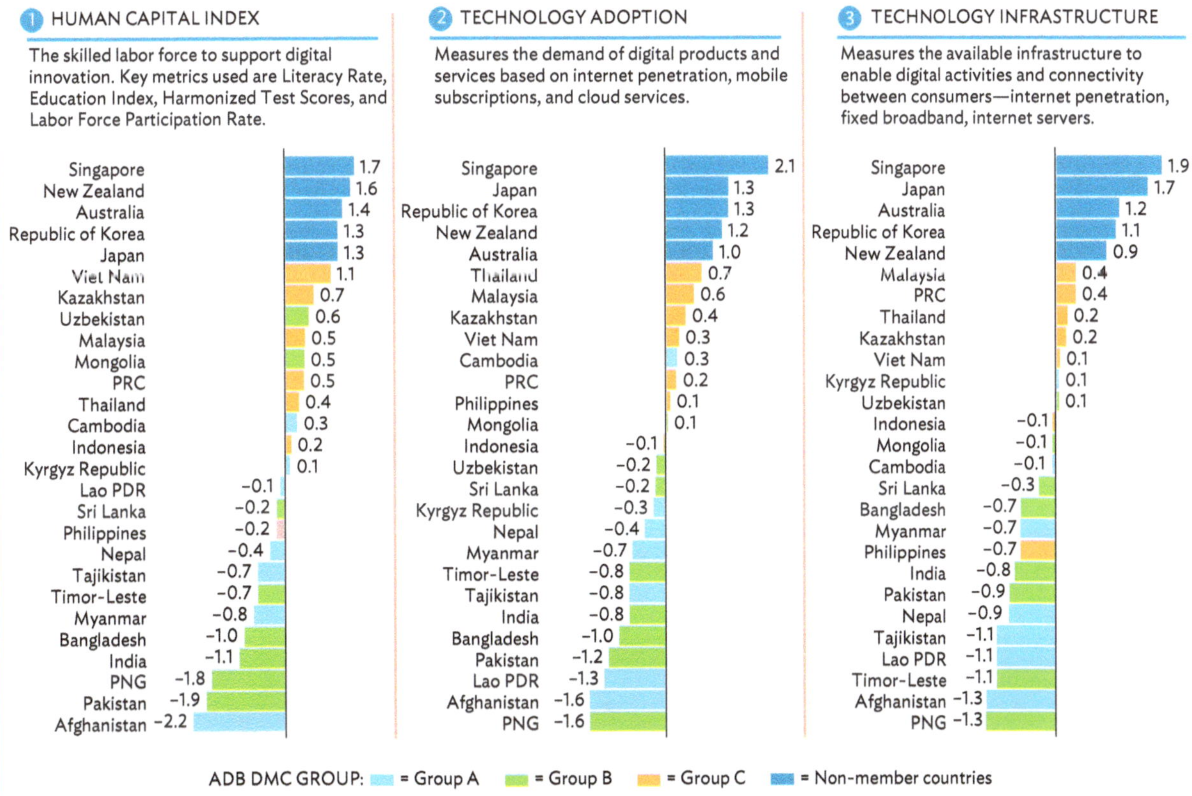

ADB = Asian Development Bank, PRC = People's Republic of China, DMC = developing member country, Lao PDR = Lao People's Democratic Republic, PNG = Papua New Guinea.

Source: Cisco Digital Readiness Index. 2021. https://www.cisco.com/c/en/us/about/csr/research-resources/digital-readiness.html.

- **Most digital twins are of maturity levels 1–3.** As of 2024, most applications of digital twins in the market are of maturity levels 1–3 (Figure A5.3), with none that exhibited characteristics of a maturity level 4 or 5 digital twin (in accordance with the maturity levels defined in Section 1.5). This skewed distribution may be because the maturity level of the digital twin that is implemented is highly dependent on several factors such as budget availability, time, technical capacity, data infrastructure, and data and other requirements. As expected, it was observed that developed countries with higher digital readiness also exhibited more mature digital twins.

Figure A5.3: Digital Twins by Level of Maturity, by Region

MATURITY LEVEL BY REGION

Currently for infrastructure- and asset-based digital twins, Level 3 maturity levels are indicatively the highest complexity of digital twins seen.

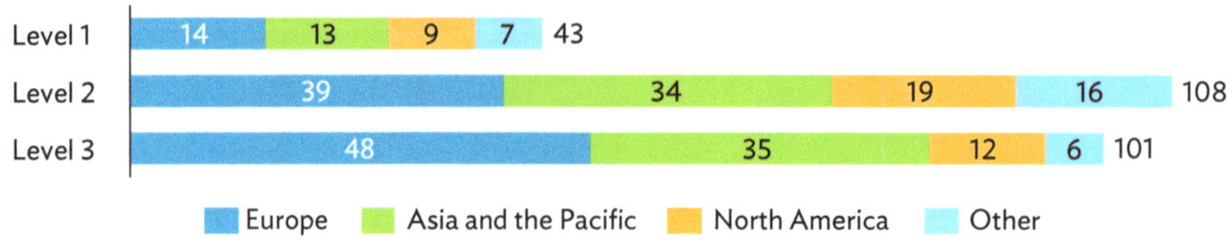

Source: Author.

- **Key enabling technologies in digital twins were mainly data modeling and visualization, cloud computing, and Internet of Things (IoT).** In alignment with the maturity levels of the digital twins observed in the use-case library, the most common enabling technologies were those that supported digital twins of maturity levels 1–3, including data modeling and visualization and IoT. Data modeling and visualization was used in almost all digital twin use-cases, whereas IoT, spatial computing, and cloud computing were as prevalent in many use-cases. Many of these technologies were also packaged within pre-built software and platforms across most use-cases. As expected, artificial intelligence (AI) and machine learning were only seen in 35% of the digital twins—with most being at maturity level 3 and above. The most common enabling technologies were also shared among the top three sectors (Figure A5.4).

Figure A5.4: Application of Enabling Technologies in Digital Twins by Sector

ENABLING TECHNOLOGIES BY SECTOR

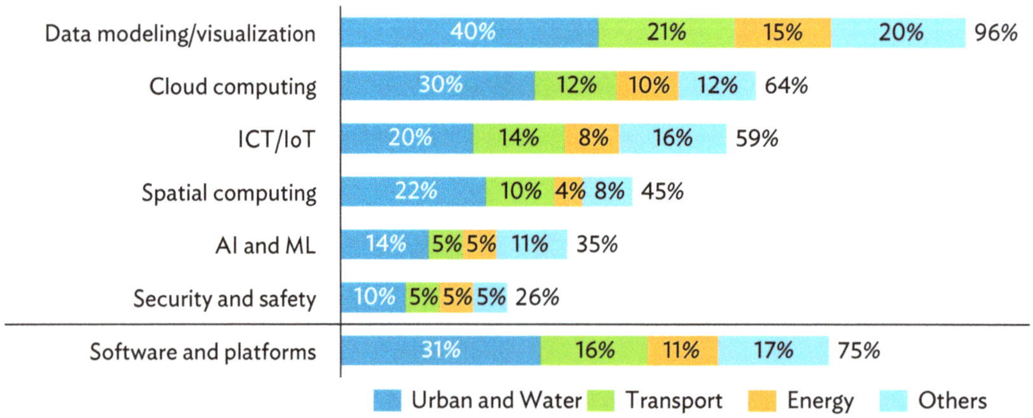

AI = artificial intelligence, ICT = information and communication technology, IoT = Internet of Things, ML = machine learning.
Source: Author.

- **Benefits sought from digital twins were mainly around informed decision-making, visualization and monitoring, improving operations and maintenance (O&M), and improvements in productivity.** For both public and private stakeholders, recognizing the potential to address inefficiencies and decision-making in developing resilient infrastructure or other uses, and subsequently integrating these iterative solutions will enable the development of comprehensive and valuable digital twins (Figure A5.5). As the following subchapters will illustrate, potential benefits range from increased security and safety to optimizing resource loss. The four most prolific themes of added value are the ability to (i) make informed decisions, (ii) visualize and monitor the physical twin, (iii) improve O&M, and (iv) achieve gains in productivity or efficiencies. These four are maintained across key sectors.

Figure A5.5: Digital Twin Use-Cases by Key Benefits

Source: Based on an AWR Lloyd analysis.

- **Typical traits of maturity levels 1 and 2 digital twins:** An analysis of the use-cases reveals the following:

Maturity Level 1

» **Top three sectors:** Water and Urban Development (43%), Transport (24%), Energy (19%)
» **Top three geographies:** Europe (33%), Asia and the Pacific (31%), North America (21%)
» **Top three enabling technologies:** Data modeling and visualization (90%), software and platforms (69%), information and communication technology/IoT (62%)
» **Top three benefits:** Visualization and monitoring (74%), informed decision-making (72%), productivity gains (50%)

Maturity Level 2:

» **Top three sectors:** Water and Urban Development (51%), Transport (20%), Energy (10%)
» **Top three geographies:** Europe (36%), Asia and the Pacific (31%), North America (18%)
» **Top three enabling technologies:** Data modeling and visualization (96%), software and platforms (77%), cloud computing (75%)

Top three benefits: Informed decision-making (89%); Visualization and monitoring (84%); Improved operations, inspection, and maintenance (67%)

Appendix 6
Needs Assessment

While digital twins are gaining industry-wide traction and have the potential to serve as a tool for developing climate-adaptive and climate-resilient infrastructure, its development can be a lengthy, complex, and expensive process.

Thus, it is important to first take a step back and determine whether a digital twin is an appropriate solution for the infrastructure project and whether certain prerequisites can be satisfied by the infrastructure asset owners, operators, and other key decision-makers of the digital twin development.

Before embarking on the first step to developing a digital twin, the Asian Development Bank (ADB) project team is encouraged to complete the Needs Assessment—to check whether they have sufficient understanding of their current knowledge base, capacity, and strategic needs— before they get started on the road map. The Needs Assessment aims to conduct a preliminary evaluation to ascertain the feasibility of initiating a digital twin journey for the respective project and assesses its readiness by using three fundamental aspects—knowledge, capacity, and strategic need.

If just one enabling technology (Section 1.4) can fulfill the strategic needs, then users should consider that alternative technology.

About the Needs Assessment

The Needs Assessment assumes that the successful implementation of any digital transformation project such as a digital twin will benefit from a solid foundation, proficient working team, and strategic alignment of the goals and objectives among the relevant stakeholders.

As a result, the major determinants that contribute to the successful implementation of a digital twin can be summarized into the following three key pillars:

1. **Knowledge.** This first pillar assesses the level of understanding and awareness of digital twins and is based on the guiding question—*Does the ADB project team, as the champions of the digital twin for the infrastructure project, have sufficient knowledge to pursue a digital twin initiative?*

   The knowledge base of the ADB project team will impact the ease in which they understand the related terminologies, scope, and use-cases in designing the application for the project in the subsequent steps.

2. **Capacity.** The next pillar assesses the technical capabilities of relevant stakeholders, as well as the digital readiness of the project and the country that is implementing it. The pillar is based on the guiding question—*Does the project have the supporting enabling technologies, resources and capabilities, and infrastructure needed to deploy a digital twin?*

The technical capacity will impact the ease of deploying a digital twin in terms of the supporting enabling technologies, capabilities, and related infrastructure.

3. **Strategic need.** The last pillar assesses the goals of the project and the strategic fit of a digital twin toward fulfilling these goals.

   This pillar determines the extent to which a digital twin can increase the effectiveness of the project's intended impact and address the project country's needs. For instance, the lack of or unclear digital transformation policy in the context of the project may lead to premature or impractical implementation of the digital twin, and even to budgetary constraints.

The needs assessment tool provides recommendations to the project team to either embark on the digital twin journey or take a step back and reconsider whether a digital twin is the right solution for their project based on their knowledge, capacity, and strategic needs. It is also important to note that the recommendation is only indicative; the project team can choose to continue on the digital twin road map if there is strong conviction. The final questionnaire can be accessed here.

Appendix 7
Problem-Solution Alignment

Business needs and potential risks of development project are assessed and prioritized vis-à-vis the capabilities of digital twin. This process aims to guarantee that the digital twin or Digital Twin Lite delivers the targeted business benefits effectively, and this is presented in Figure A7.

Figure A7: Illustrative Thought Process of the Problem-Solution Alignment

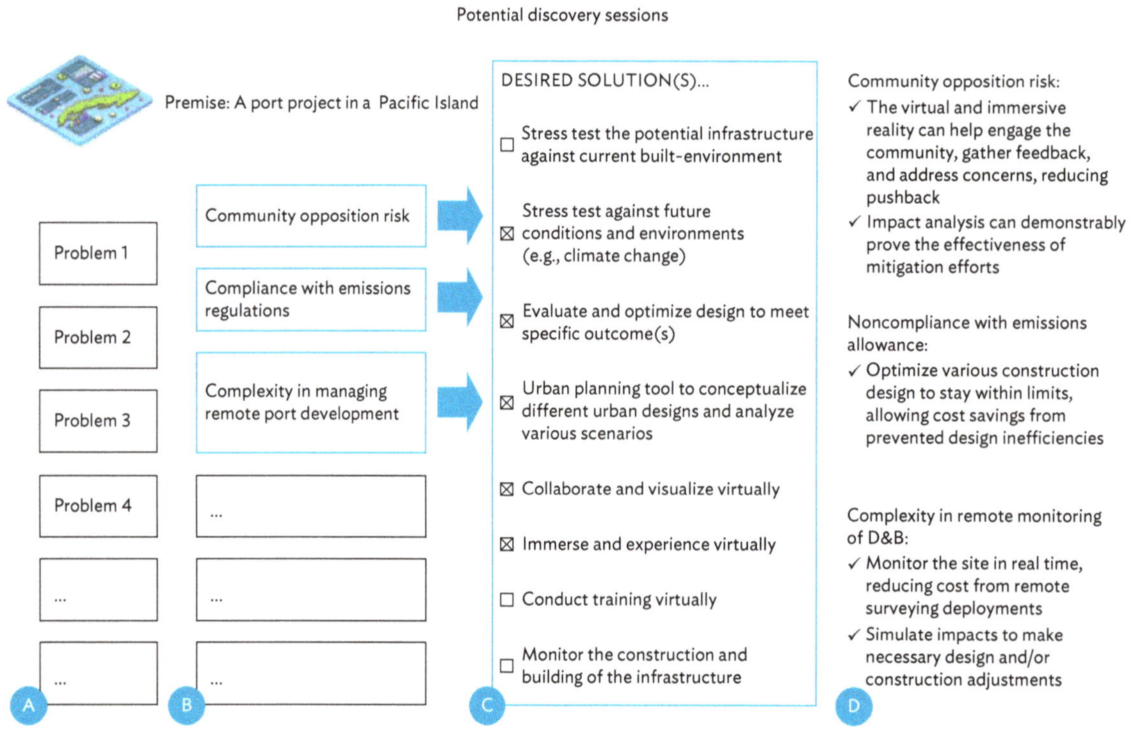

D&B = design and build.

Source: Author. Adapted from the problem statement and value proposition guidelines from the best practice digital twin development publications of the Centre for Digital Built Britain, Institute of Electrical and Electronics Engineers, University of Michigan, and other institutions.

A. Users should begin by creating a comprehensive list of currently known problems, issues, pain points, and challenges associated with the infrastructure project. This list should encompass both qualitative and quantitative aspects as much as possible.

B. Once the list is compiled, conduct a prioritization exercise to rearrange the problems so that those with high value are prominently in focus. Factors such as the severity and likelihood of each problem occurring will help with this prioritization. This step is crucial to ensure that the most critical issues are addressed first. For the considered premise, the prioritized challenges may be addressing the high cost and complexity of the port construction and monitoring due to its remote location, and thus, heightened risks of delays. Communities may be strongly opposed to the project due to lack of funding and emissions are not able to be efficiently mitigated due to the lack of knowledge.

C. After prioritizing the problems, evaluate whether technological interventions, such as digital twin, can effectively resolve these high-value problems. This evaluation should consider whether the proposed desired solutions, when paired against the prioritized problems, remain sensible and effective.

D. Lastly, the consideration of this problem–solution link should be clearly articulated to ensure that the solution is developed to support project needs and objectives, and that the chosen solution supports the project's needs and objectives effectively.

Throughout this process, consider engaging in discovery sessions or consultations with other project stakeholders. These interactions can provide valuable insights and may lead to a more exhaustive list of issues or correct prioritization, ensuring that no critical aspects are overlooked. For instance, if a detailed stakeholder assessment reveals no significant problem for the infrastructure, it may be indicative of a lack of purpose for the digital twin.

Appendix 8
Best Practice—Detailed Technical and Investment Case

This section provides information on the best practice that project teams or users can follow to build a detailed Business Case that has technical and business details broken down. To build a more detailed Technical Case for the digital twin, users will be required to answer the following guiding questions.

As with the Digital Twin Strategy Canvas, users can revisit this Step 2 and more articulately answer these questions as they progress along the digital twin road map.

- *What are the key indicators that measure the outputs and outcomes of the project?*

  Using the Design and Monitoring Framework (DMF) structure published by the Asian Development Bank (ADB), users should first identify the key performance indicators in relation to the *outputs* and *outcomes* of their project. The ADB DMF defines outputs as products or services that the project delivers to the beneficiaries, whereas outcomes are a result of outputs and the immediate and direct benefits of the project. In the context of this framework, outputs of the digital twin can be informed by the "Desired Solution(s) and Benefits" in the Digital Twin Strategy Canvas, and outcomes can be inferred from the expected functionality and benefits.

  The achievement of both outputs and outcomes is measured through *performance indicators*. Performance indicators provide a measurable basis for project monitoring and evaluation. Each performance indicator must have a baseline and a target; should be tagged to a corresponding operational priority (OP) indicator; should be specific, measurable, achievable, relevant, and time-bound (SMART); and should be *direct indicators* but can be one of any three types of indicators, as follows:

  - **Direct indicators** directly measure the subject of interest and should be used whenever feasible. For example, the number of fatalities from road accidents annually is a direct indicator of the outcome statement "reduced deaths from road traffic accidents."
  - **Proxy indicators** indirectly measure the subject of interest and is appropriate when direct measures are not feasible. For example, poor housing quality may be used as proxy indicators of poverty.
  - **Leading indicators** measure preliminary indications of an outcome by measuring progress along the pathway of change. For example, the number of workshop participants indicating their willingness to apply newly learned skills may be used as a leading indicator for their actual application of the skills.

  As an example, the appropriate output, outcome, and performance indicator for ADB's road design case study in Uzbekistan could be as follows:

  Example of output, outcome, and performance indicator

  - ***Output:*** *Digital twin analyzes the alternative road designs carbon emissions*
  - ***Outcome:*** *Digital twin improves road sustainability*

- *__Performance indicator:__ Significant reduction of at least 15% of road designs carbon emissions (kilograms of carbon dioxide equivalent [kgCO2e]) compared against the base case design of nearly 40 million kgCO2e.*

• *What are the data requirements for the key indicators?*

Continuing along ADB's DMF structure, use the performance indicators to identify the required data and related data collection methods. Data requirements encompass interactions among the digital twin, asset, and connected stakeholder or interface. This ecosystem is informed by the Digital Twin Strategy Canvas and the process of completing it.

Users can begin to map out the required data relationships to anticipate the level of involvement from different stakeholders by asking: *What data is required?' and How will it be collected?*

- To understand the **data requirements**, users should first ask what data can most accurately or suitably measure the indicator being assessed and the source of data or where to retrieve it. In the absence of data that directly measures the indicator, the next best alternatives should be outlined. For example, measuring the carbon footprint of an infrastructure project design prototype may require data on recognized carbon emission rates of available construction materials, such as cement.
- When determining the source, users should also consider the different data types (mobile, environmental, financial, and others) and time aspects (historical, present, or projections) available. For example, historical measurements of local precipitation data from local organizations may be a required dataset to accurately understand the virtual design's interactions with the local environment. Users are encouraged to be as specific as possible when defining data requirements.
- As the next step, consider the **data collection** approach for each of the identified data. This will involve identifying the relevant interface (technology, human, hybrid), frequency (real time, near real time, monthly), and if it is primary or secondary (project collected, existing datasets). The most appropriate method should both collect quality data for the indicator and be feasible. Collection methods for DMF indicators often include reviews of existing documentation, observation, surveys and/or interviews, and physical measurements.

As an example, some of the data requirements for the road design case study in Uzbekistan could be as follows:

Examples of data requirements

- *__Data requirements.__ Carbon emission factor of cement (energy to produce) sourced from local cement plants and ORIS Materials Intelligence platform; quantities of cement used for different road designs from design specifications (current project, SETRA 98, RStO 12).*
- *__Data collection.__ Site survey to confirm material production and energy usage, review of local and international datasets for material carbon footprints, and review of European road standards for road design specifications.*

• *What are the enabling technologies for the key indicators?*

Data requirements should help users infer the enabling technologies necessary for two goals: the collection and use or manipulation of data to achieve the digital twin's functionality—defined earlier as outputs. For example, following the data through its transformation can involve considerations on (i) data storage (local, cloud), (ii) its processing (analytics, modeling), and (iii) how it is ultimately presented or used (user interfaces, web portals, apps).

Users are recommended to base key enabling technologies from the list used in the Use-Case Library and build or elaborate upon it as necessary. If any difficulties are met, the maturity level identified in the Digital Twin Strategy Canvas can inform the baseline key technologies, which are required to achieve the level's defined functionality.

For example, some of the enabling technologies for the Uzbekistan case study may be as follows:

Examples of enabling technologies

- ☒ *Data modeling and visualization—to calculate road design emissions (output)*
- ☐ *Information and communication technology (ICT) and Internet of Things (IoT)*
- ☒ *Artificial intelligence and/or machine learning—to analyze data and carbon emissions on alternative road designs (output)*
- ☒ *Spatial computing (computer-aided design, geographic information system, global positioning system, global navigation satellite system)*
- ☐ *Cloud computing*
- ☒ *Software and platforms (Global Cement and Concrete Association calculation tool and ORIS Carbon Calculator; ORIS Materials Intelligence platform)*
- ☐ *Security and safety*
- ☐ *Others*

Building the Business Case

With the Digital Twin Strategy Canvas and Technical Case completed, users should now have a foundational understanding of the expected functionality, maturity level, benefits, and purpose of the digital twin. Also, users should already have an idea of the enabling technologies that the digital twin will leverage for the collection and processing of the data required to assess the key performance indicators of the project.

At this point, the Business Case will provide a preliminary answer whether a digital twin or Digital Twin Lite should be developed or not by evaluating the cost–benefit analysis or return on investment (ROI) analysis. Although project teams can use the ROI model as a template for this analysis, the details will have to be consolidated and inputted into the relevant "override" fields.

- *What are the key benefits achieved from implementing this digital twin?*

  Quantifying the incremental direct benefits of the digital twin, both tangible and intangible, over its operating life cycle is crucial to justify its investment. Users should derive the expected benefits from the Digital Twin Strategy Canvas and the key performance indicators from the Technical Case, and refer to the potential benefits from use-cases in their sector (Appendix 2).

  Tangible benefits are benefits that are quantifiable and measurable, such as the number of labor hours or the amount of cost reduction, which can more precisely be assigned a monetary value. On the other hand, intangible benefits—such as improved customer satisfaction, social well-being, and reducing carbon footprint—have a subjective monetary value. Finally, incremental benefits means that it assesses the benefits with and without the digital twin.

  Several methods can be used by users to quantify the economic prices of benefits. Users can also refer to ADB's *Guidelines for the Economic Analysis of Projects*, which provides a benefit valuation by sector, and discusses in detail the method for valuing project benefits in the major sectors of ADB operations.

An example of benefits using the Uzbekistan road design case could be as follows:

Examples of direct benefits

- ***Carbon emissions in base case (without digital twin):*** *39,800 tons of carbon dioxide equivalent (tCO2e)*
- ***Carbon emission with alternative design (with digital twin):*** *37,200 tCO2e*
- ***Economic price of carbon:*** *$40/tCO2e*
- ***Incremental benefits:*** *reduction of 2,600 tCO2e or reduction in the social cost of carbon by $104,000*

- *What are the costs associated with developing and implementing this digital twin?*

Users should determine the high-level financial requirements using ADB's publication on *Cost Estimation in Sovereign Operations* as a guide. This publication defines a "cost estimate" as an approximation of a project's probable cost, which consists of the base cost, contingencies, and financial charges during implementation. For digital twins, the base cost should be the focus of the cost estimation, represented by both capital and operating expenditures. To estimate the total cost of ownership of a digital twin, which is often informed by anticipated budgets and revisited with expert consultation, it can be broken down into the following:

- **Capital expenditures (CAPEX).** This reflects hardware, software, and/or personnel capital enhancements informed by the enabling technologies that were identified to achieve digital twin's output. It may also include other technologies that add value or synergy to the digital twin's purpose as defined in the canvas. CAPEX should be broken down through essential elements of the makeup of a specific enabling technology. For example, the use of Internet of Things (IoT) may require sensor costs per unit type, quantity, and installation costs.
- **Operating expenditures (OPEX).** This will involve longer-term cost implications to maintain the digital twin's achievement of outputs and outcomes. For example, OPEX may be associated with servicing, upskilling, maintenance, or data and/or cloud hosting and analytics.
- **Other expenses.** This should consider indirect and miscellaneous costs of the digital twin. For example, other expenses may include budgets for contingencies and unexpected financial charges, or costs related to regulatory compliance.

The overall cost for developing and implementing a digital twin will scale with its complexity and size. Users should revisit the Digital Twin Strategy Canvas to ensure that resulting cost estimates fully reflect the desired functionalities but remain within defined limitations. An ROI result that is outside acceptable ranges may likely be due to digital twins that are too complex and costly. Reevaluating technological alternatives and quotations can assist in this process.

An example of costs using the Uzbekistan road design case could be as follows:

Examples of partial associated costs

- ***CAPEX:*** *ORIS platform license, data analytics, and machine learning software at $20,000 (Basic digital twin software costs); Data analyst personnel for 2 months at $8,000/month; Satellite image recognition for 25 square kilometers at $10/square kilometer*
- ***OPEX:*** *No estimated OPEX until the digital twin is connected with operational data*
- ***Others:*** *Cost of dataset acquisition for embedded carbon emissions*

Appendix 9
List of Technology Providers

In general, digital twin technology providers can offer a range of products or services that comprises different scales and complexities—a singular product and/or platform as an element, specific services, or a full suite that covers the end-to-end process of developing, implementing, and maintaining a digital twin. A detailed library of technology providers that provide digital twin or complementary products and services can be found in this Technology Provider Database. Do note that the database is not exhaustive and should not be considered as recommendations from the Asian Development Bank (ADB).

Product and/or Platform

Technology providers can offer various proprietary software that gives their clients (often a *Service Provider)* the option to build different types of digital twins depending on the end-user's requirements. These products can range from building information modeling (BIM) to 3D modeling software; they do not necessarily provide services that will help end users adopt and operate the digital twin solution. Examples of technology providers include Amazon Web Services (AWS), Autodesk, Dassault Systèmes, Skycatch, and Tygron.

Service Provider

Service providers can offer systems integration and consultation services in the field of technology and engineering. These technology partners assume a leading role in delivering projects and managing the assets of their clients (digital twin end users) and typically provide such services across all project development cycles—from conceptual to the operational stage. Some key services include modeling and documentation of an asset using a designated *Product/Platform* and conducting capacity-building sessions for end users. Examples of service providers include Atlas Industries and Mott MacDonald.

End-to-End

Partners in this area provide a fully-fledged digital twin solution both in *Product/Platform* and *Services*. End-to-end technology partners are cross cutting in that they provide readiness assessment and capacity-building sessions that complement their in-house *Product/Platform*, ensuring that end users are enabled for digitalization. Notable examples include AVEVA, AWS, Bentley, and Dassault Systèmes.

Some end-to-end providers are listed in the table below. Do note that these are only examples and should not be considered as recommendations from ADB.

Technology Providers with Digital Twin Services	
Name	**Headquarters**
1Spatial	United Kingdom
3D Repo	United Kingdom
51World	People's Republic of China
Aras	United States
Accenture	Ireland
AccuCities	United Kingdom
Advanced Infrastructure	United Kingdom
Akademiska Hus	Sweden
Akselos	Switzerland
ALIM Systems	United Kingdom
AlmavivA S.p.A.	Italy
Altair	United States
Amazon Web Services	United States
Amberg Group AG	Switzerland
AMC Bridge LLC	United States
Ansys	United States
AnyLogic	United States
Arup	United Kingdom
AsiaInfo	People's Republic of China
Atlas Industries	Guernsey
Aurecon	Australia
Autodesk	United States
Aveva	United Kingdom
Beamo	Republic of Korea
Bentley Systems	United States
Berkeley & Imperial	United States
BRIDG	United States
BT Group	United Kingdom
Buildots	Israel
Buro Happold	United Kingdom
C9VT	United Kingdom
CFMS Services	United Kingdom
CMCL Innovations	United Kingdom
CSIRO, Data 61	Australia
Cohesive	United States
Cognite	Norway
Costain	United Kingdom
DASSAULT SYSTÈMES	France
DataMesh	Singapore

Table continued

Table continued

Technology Providers with Digital Twin Services	
Name	**Headquarters**
Decision Lab	United Kingdom
DNV	United Kingdom
Duality	United States
E8ight	Republic of Korea
Elliott Wood	United Kingdom
Emu Analytics	United Kingdom
Envirosuite	Australia
Eos Positioning Systems	Canada
ESRI	United States
Faculty Science	United Kingdom
FARO Technologies	United States
Fathom	Saudi Arabia
Fintricity	United States
Framatome	France
Fujitsu	Japan
Fusion242	United Kingdom
General Electric	United States
Getmapping	United Kingdom
Giraffe	Australia
Graffiquo	Singapore
High-Performance Computing Center Stuttgart	Germany
Hitachi	Japan
IBM	United States
IES	Scotland
Iliad Consortium	N/A
IMERZA	United States
Invicara	Ireland
IOTICS	United Kingdom
Jacobs	United States
Jungle AI	Portugal
Kaiasm	United Kingdom
KCI	United States
KEO	Kuwait
Kepco E&C	Canada
Krellian	United Kingdom
Leica Geosystems	Switzerland
LEMAUREY	United Kingdom
Luniq	United Kingdom

Table continued

Table continued

Technology Providers with Digital Twin Services	
Name	**Headquarters**
MathWorks	United States
Matterport	United States
Microsoft Azure	United States
MindEarth	Switzerland
Mott MacDonald	United Kingdom
NavVis	Germany
National Instruments Corp.	United States
Neuron	Hong Kong, China
Nokia Systems	Finland
Nomoko	Switzerland
NTT Data	Japan
NVIDIA	United States
Oak Ridge National Laboratory	N/A
OpenSpace	United States
ORIS	France
Palantir Technologies	United States
Pointerra3D	Australia
PTC	United States
Ramboll	Denmark
Razor	United Kingdom
RemSense	Australia
Royal HaskoningDHV	Netherlands
SAP	Germany
Sedaro	United States
Semantic Arts	United States
Sensat	United Kingdom
Siemens	Germany
Siradel	France
Skycatch	United States
Slingshot Simulations	United Kingdom
Softengi	Ukraine
Spinview	United Kingdom
SuperMap	People's Republic of China
Tekuchi	United Kingdom
Texas A&M Engineering Experiment Station	United States
Th3rdcurve	United Kingdom
The Boundary	United Kingdom
The National Institute of Water and Atmospheric Research	New Zealand

Table continued

Table continued

Technology Providers with Digital Twin Services	
Name	**Headquarters**
Thridium	United Kingdom
TIS INTEC Group	Japan
Topcon Positioning Group	United States
Twinview	United Kingdom
Tygron	Netherlands
UINO	People's Republic of China
Unity	United States
Unreal Engine	United States
Urban Hawk	United Kingdom
Varadise Limited	Hong Kong, China
VirtualSpaces	United States
Visco	Japan
VTT	Finland

Source: Author's analysis.

Appendix 10
Gemini Principles

The Gemini Principles were developed by the Centre for Digital Built Britain to aid in the development of a National Digital Twin. The principles were designed to lay the groundwork for contextualizing the intended purpose of a digital twin, guiding users with questions that can be identified and addressed. These are also descriptive and applicable to all solutions, which encourages flexibility for innovation and development. Ultimately, the principles are intended to help in developing digital twins that are to be strategically aligned to allow each twin to be part of a larger whole (in its context, the National Digital Twin). For more details, see the Centre for Digital Built Britain's report on the Gemini principles.

There are nine principles organized under three main pillars, each with key premises and points, as follows:

Purpose

The digital twin must have a clear and transparent purpose to help improve outcomes throughout its operational period. These intentions aim to improve both aspects of the underlying project, as well as indirect economic, social, environmental, safety, and security outcomes. The outcomes will need to be substantiated with evidence and have to be disseminated across all relevant stakeholders. These can be broken into the following principles:

1. **Public Good**

The digital twin should ultimately deliver genuine and perpetual benefits, starting with the users' needs and moving toward inclusive economic, social, and environmental benefits for the public.

2. **Value Creation**

The digital twin should generate sustainable value at asset, process, and system levels such as performance improvements and effective risk management. This will facilitate greater economic value, promote innovation and competition, and allow benefits to be accessible.

3. **Insight**

The digital twin must be able to provide measurable insights into the built environment, enabling informed decision-making and ultimately resulting in better outcomes.

Trust

The digital twin must be publicly trustworthy; "ethical by design;" and compliant with transparent regulatory oversight, ethical standards, and/or related frameworks. Digital twins' constant transmission and use of data introduces the need for security and trustworthiness. Trust in the digital twin ultimately impacts stakeholders' willingness to contribute to the quality and effectiveness of insights that the twin produces.

4. **Security**

The digital twin must follow data security protocols and standards provided by best practices from industries and nations, and enable security of data privacy, intellectual property, and more.

5. **Openness**

The digital twin must be as transparent as possible while maintaining the principles set out in *Security* to ensure that there is a balance between integrity and *Quality*. Open data, culture of collaboration, adherence standards, and utilization of open-source approaches are critical.

6. **Quality**

The data from which the digital twin is being built must be of suitable quality for its intended purpose to facilitate informed decision-making and provide security and longevity for the system.

Function

The digital twin must be functional and effective in addressing its intended purposes and is publicly available to users to ensure availability when needed. A key enabler for the functionality and trustworthiness of digital twins is the secure interoperability of data and its management.

7. **Federation**

The digital twin should adhere to an information management framework, emphasizing best interoperability practices to ensure it is based on a standard and connected environment. They must be able to work with different data classes across various sectors and built environments.

8. **Curation**

The digital twin must demonstrate a clear ownership of data, be able to manage the governance of the ecosystem, and incentivize favorable regulatory forces to promote accountability.

9. **Evolution**

The digital twin should be built to adapt and develop as technology, society, requirements, information management, cybersecurity, and the built environment evolves.

Appendix 11
About SPADE

What is SPADE?

The Spatial Data Analysis Explorer (SPADE) is a web-based, open-source platform on a centralized cloud-based server containing various geospatial data that can be utilized for project identification and preparation, due diligence, engineering design, project monitoring, and analysis of climate change impacts on projects.[2] The platform was developed for the Asian Development Bank (ADB) under the Urban Climate Change Resilience Trust Fund in 2018. Baseline data are gathered from different sources, such as earth observation and meteorological satellite data, hydrometeorological data, and climate change simulations from the Data Integration and Analysis System hosted by the University of Tokyo. Socioeconomic data are also collected from field surveys and a mobile application for data collection made by the Asian Institute of Technology. Currently, SPADE contains spatial information of over 1,100 layers and 100 maps of the geographic information system (GIS) data for 21 project cities in seven countries across Asia.[3]

How is it used?

SPADE aims to support the preparation of climate risk, vulnerability, and urban system assessments that can inform the development of regional and urban master plans and strategies, as well as identify opportunities to enhance the performance of infrastructure investments. This technology allows users to combine and compare different climate change scenarios with land use and infrastructure datasets that can inform project design and implementation processes and strengthen resilience across urban systems and sectors.[3]

What is its relevance to digital twins?

Digital twins require different forms of datasets like building information modeling (BIM) and Internet of Things (IOT) sensors, thus, a platform is needed as a base repository. To facilitate this, SPADE could potentially integrate the different datasets and base maps supporting the digital twin technology. There are current efforts to institutionalize the platform within ADB. SPADE was presented at the Digital Twin Workshop in Singapore and the Digital Management Sub Committee at ADB headquarters. Both presentations were supported by the Office of Information System Technology Division. In addition, SPADE could also be a repository of geospatial datasets produced by projects within ADB. Currently, there is no repository of GIS datasets, which means future projects would either recreate or repurchase the needed geospatial information.[3]

2 GeoNode Summit. 2019. ADB SPADE.

3 ADB. 2021. Catalyzing Innovation and Digitization for Safe, Sustainable, Resilient, and Inclusive Water Management.

SPADE Pilot Projects in La Trinidad, Philippines and Hue, Viet Nam

The Spatial Data Analysis Explorer (SPADE) was piloted in five project cities in Bangladesh (Bagerhat and Patuakhali) and Viet Nam (Ha Ghiang, Hue, and Vinh Yen) when it was first introduced. As of 2024, SPADE contains various datasets for 21 cities in Bangladesh, Cambodia, the People's Republic of China, India, Pakistan, the Philippines, and Viet Nam.

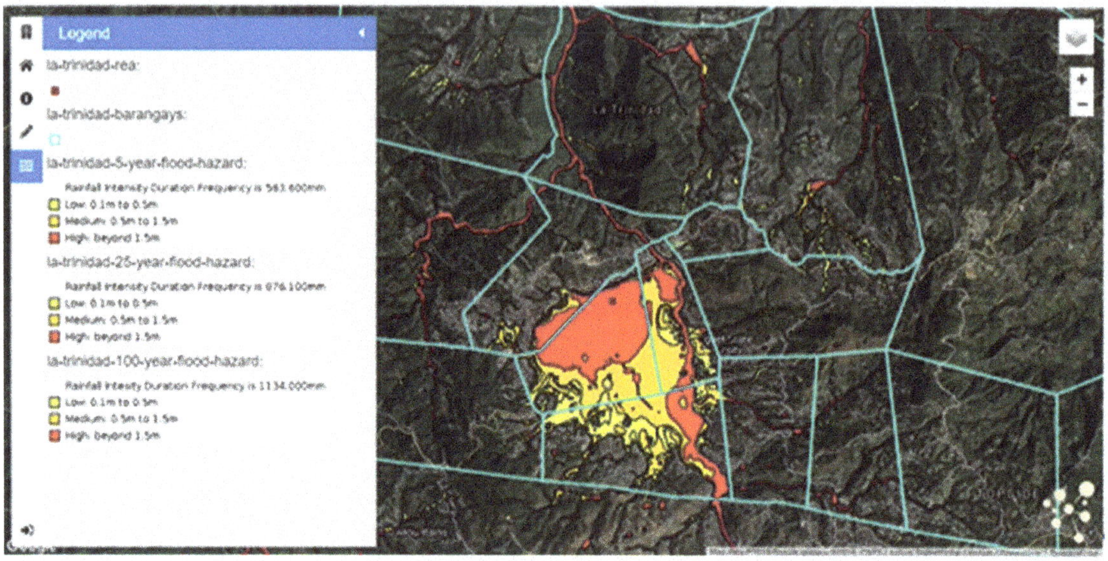

Flood hazard shown as hazard layers is overlayed over La Trinidad map.

Simple analysis function comparing scenarios for flood depth over Hue map.

Source: ADB SPADE.

Appendix 12
About DestinE

What is DestinE?

Destination Earth (DestinE) is an initiative of the European Commission to develop a digital twin for the whole planet earth with the objective of being a tool for monitoring, simulating, and predicting the interactions between natural phenomena and human activities. This initiative was launched in January 2021 to achieve the objectives of the twin transition, green and digital, as part of the European Commission's Green Deal and Digital Strategy.[4]

The DestinE system will provide evidence-based decision-making tools, applications, and services based on an open, flexible, and secure cloud-based computing infrastructure. All main components of the system—i.e., Core Service Platform, Data Lake, Digital Twin Engine—are expected to be developed by 2024. By that date, the Core Service Platform and Data Lake will be transferred into operation, as well as the demonstration of the first two digital twins on Weather-Induced Extremes and Climate Change Adaptation, and the open core platform. The DestinE Data Lake (DEDL) will bring together data from ESA, EUMETSAT, ECMWF, and from Copernicus, which will allow discovery and data access and big data processing in the cloud.

What is its relevance to digital twins?

The platform will be the integration of at least 4–5 operational digital twins, and indicatively by 2025, will be opened to the public sector for them to be able to develop, monitor, and assess the impact on the environment and climate of the policy and legislative measures. Through the convergence of the digital twins already offered through the platform by 2030, DestinE will be developed as a full digital replica of the whole planet earth.[5]

This very precise digital model of the earth would enable different user groups, such as public groups and scientific and private communities, to monitor and simulate natural and human activity, and to develop test scenarios to better predict the effects of climate change. With the current climate change challenge, this initiative is very relevant. Using DestinE modeling, it will unlock the potential of digital modeling of the earth's physical resources and related phenomena—such as climate change, marine environments, polar areas, the cryosphere, and others on a global scale—to speed up the green transition and help plan for major environmental degradation and disasters.

4 European Commission. 2023. *Destination Earth | Shaping Europe's Digital Future.*

5 European Commission. 2020. Workshop reports on Elements of Digital Twins on "Weather-induced and Geophysical Extremes" and "Climate Change Adaptation."

DestinE Potential Applications

Selected potential applications demonstrate the capabilities of the DestinE infrastructure to provide actionable data and decision support to its users. They are as follows:

1. **Application:** Supporting policy and decision-makers in decreasing pollution and optimizing routes in polar regions.
   Solutions: Accurate, high-resolution data and predictive insights will greatly enhance the safety of life and property at sea, reducing the risks associated with ice navigation. By providing more efficient route optimization, it will cut fuel consumption and emissions, contributing to the global fight against climate change, and ensure the protection of vulnerable polar ecosystems. The integration of the DestinE Core Service Platform data and machine learning algorithms will enhance the creation and dissemination of sea ice charts and other navigational tools, while significantly improving the spatial and temporal resolution of crucial data

2. **Application:** Supporting decision-makers in assessing climate-related challenges and their impact on urban areas.
   Solutions: (a) Flooding forecast—Users will have access to a full environment for forecasting, the flood risk in their territory over a certain period from the initial conditions. (b) Air pollution and air quality—Users will have the past and present view of the pollution in their territory and its comparison to the World Health Organization standards. The demonstrator will integrate examples of relevant policies (e.g., transforming roads into walking streets, Low Emission Zone deployment, and others) to support decision-making and "what-if" scenario simulations.

Source: European Commission. n.d. Destination Earth.

Appendix 13
The Future of Digital Twins in Asia and the Pacific

A. Overview of the Global Market and in Asia and the Pacific

Digital twins have exhibited rapid growth in city development and urban planning in recent years. It is predicted that by 2030, the application of digital twins will save $280 billion for urban planning, construction, and operations (ABI Research 2021). Furthermore, a global survey report revealed that 69% of the respondents in advanced industries are already applying digital twins in their operations (Altair n.d.). In terms of market size, the digital twin market for urban development is expected to exceed $48 billion by 2026, growing at a 58% compound annual growth rate (MarketsAndMarkets n.d.) (Figure A13.1).

Figure A13.1: Forecasted Market Size of Global Digital Twin Cities

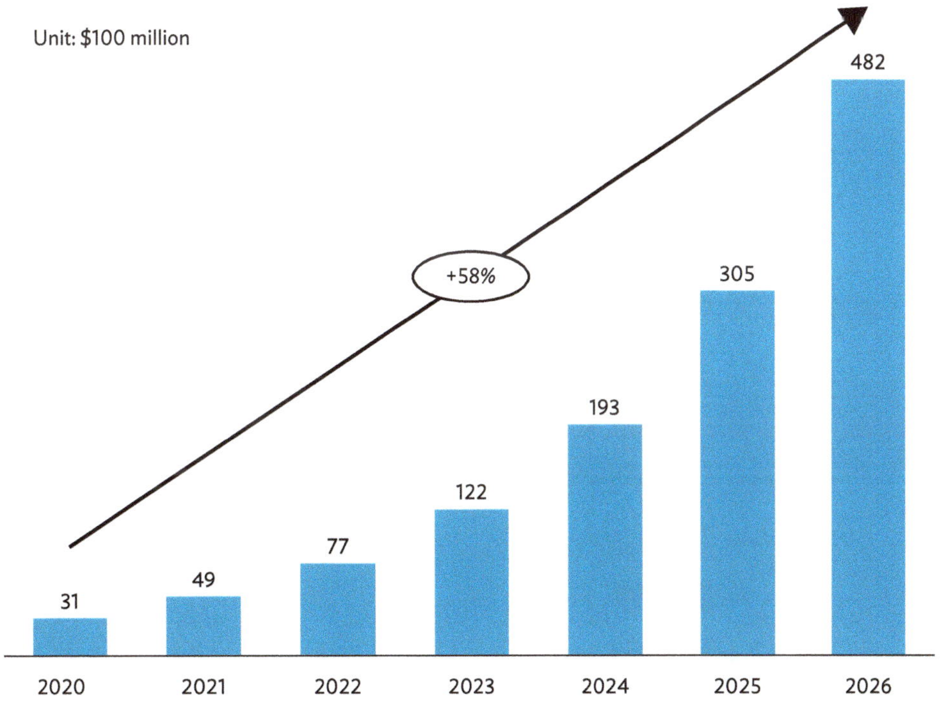

Source: World Economic Forum. 2022. Digital Twin Cities: Framework and Global Practices: INSIGHT REPORT.

This substantial growth prompted the emergence of various industry players including those that are highly specialized in select enabling technologies, applications, or sectors, as well as those that are highly integrated offering end-to-end solutions. A myriad of entities has been formed in the swift expansion, encompassing diverse services and specializations.

Although digital twin applications are substantially more prevalent in the European Union, the market size in Asia and the Pacific exceeded $1 billion in 2019 and is an increasingly attractive area for the market due to its high infrastructure growth. The region showcases some significant digital twin projects implemented in the past couple of years. The China Railway Design Corporation utilized digital twins to optimize large-scale railway design, the Jakarta to Bandung High-Speed Railway project for instance. In Singapore, their Smart City Digital Twin virtually replicates the nation and exhibits real-time dynamic data.

Nearly two-thirds of digital twin city projects globally are funded by governmental investment, hence, social capital and enterprise investment still need to be improved for digital twins to become mainstream. Precedent analysis of digital twin projects in the Asia and the Pacific region also reveals that, in general, many of Asia and the Pacific's digital twins are led by the public sector, focusing primarily on smart cities, rail, water access, and energy (see Appendix 5 for more details). Although private sector digital twins are also common in water and energy, they are spread in other applications such as facilities, construction, and manufacturing. Notably, however, many were developed by the likes of Dassault Systèmes, Bentley, Arup, and Leica, and the emergence of major players originating from the Asia and the Pacific region are yet to be observed.

It is estimated that the digital twin market in Asia and the Pacific will grow at a 35% compound annual growth rate in the coming decade, reaching a market size of $35 billion by 2030 (Fortune Business Insights n.d.). Some reports cite that digital twins for the financial services and the insurance market alone could reach $730 million by 2030 (Databridge Market Research 2023). Surveys on market sentiments suggest Asia and the Pacific as a region is more receptive to leveraging digital twin solutions in its businesses compared to other regions. Although currently, Australia dominates the digital twin market, followed by the People's Republic of China and other economies in East Asia, economies like Indonesia, the Philippines, and Thailand hold promising growth potential in the years ahead (Figure A13.2).

Figure A13.2: Digital Twin Implementation in Asia and the Pacific, Based on Use-Case Library

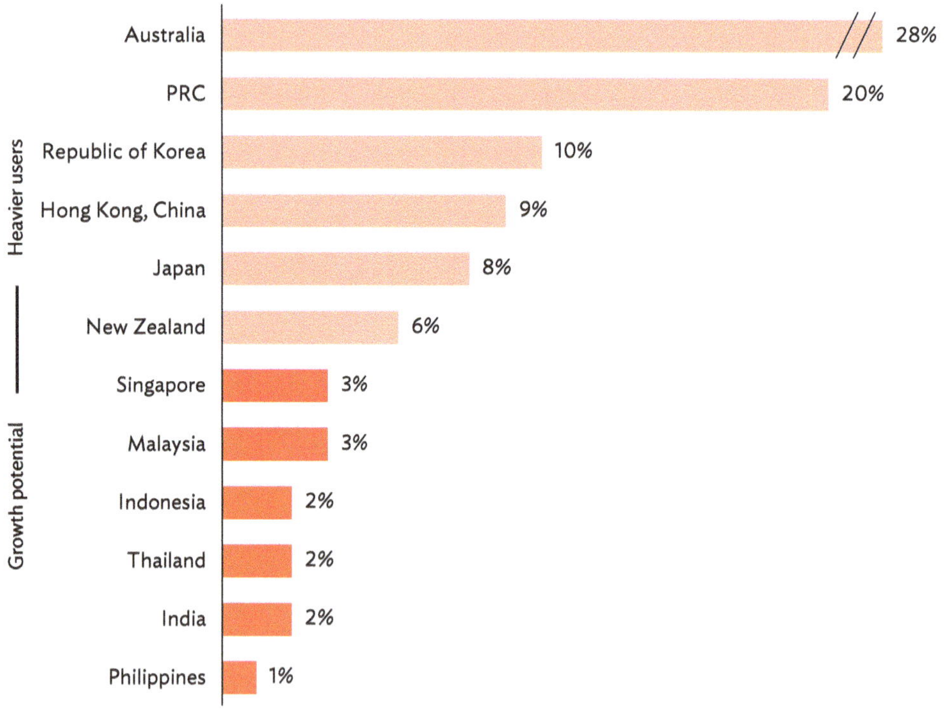

PRC = People's Republic of China.
Source: Author. Adapted from the Use-Case Library.

B. Evolution and Horizon for the Future of Digital Twins

The evolution of digital twins over the past century can be best described as the transition from "static to smart," initially demonstrated through simulations of static datasets and basic monitoring systems to technologies featuring real-time connectivity and automation (Figure A13.3). This transition is enabled by higher levels of data integration and computational power.

Figure A13.3: The Evolution of Digital Twins

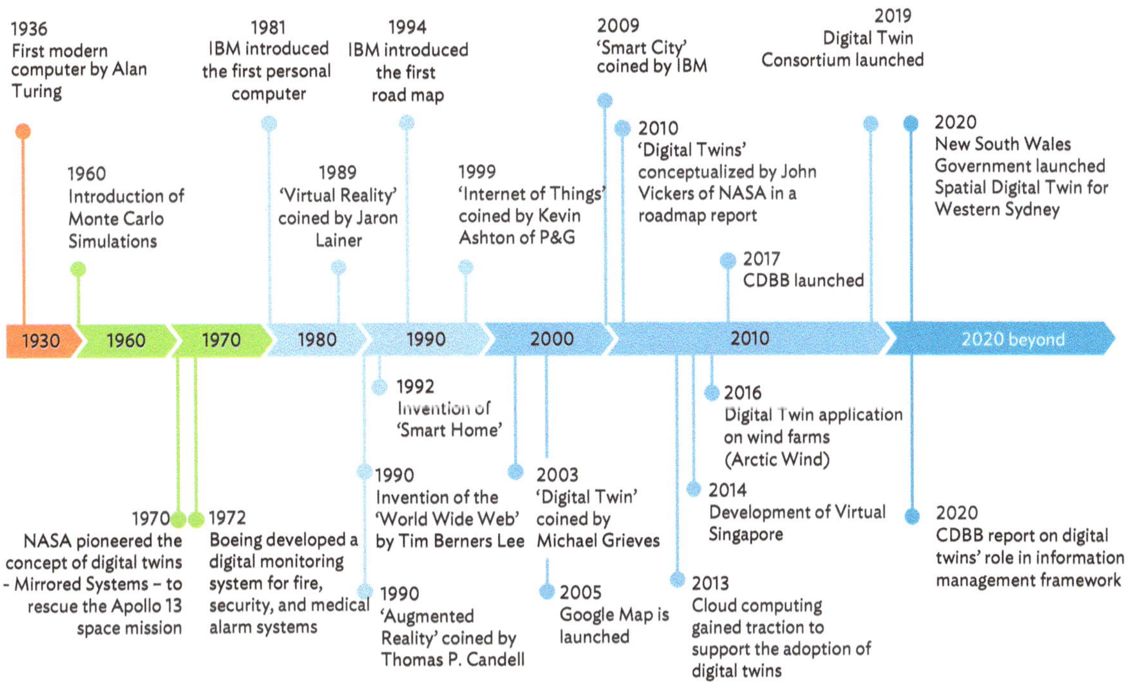

CDBB = Centre for Digital Built Britain, NASA = National Aeronautics and Space Administration

Sources: Global Data thematic research on digital twins and Arup Digital Twin Framework.

The global landscape for digital twins has seen an accelerated pace of innovation mainly through advancements in big data, high network speeds enabling cloud computing, artificial intelligence (AI), and supercomputing. The unfolding landscape of technological innovation presents possibilities that are yet to be fully comprehended—the potential applications of digital twins transcend the bounds of human imagination.

In the realm of engineering, digital twins emerge as a transformative force. In aircraft engineering, collaborative efforts between industry leaders and the academia look to revolutionize the design of intelligent aircraft fleets by integrating physics-based models with interpretable machine learning. This particular project holds promise of advancing the safety of unmanned aerial vehicles, which will certainly have commercial applications in the future (Kapteyn et al. 2020).

As exemplified by the historical context of Apollo 13, digital twins will continue to play a pivotal role in space exploration. They provide solutions to unexpected challenges, particularly for missions extending beyond the current limits of feasibility in terms of distance and duration. Digital twins are further hypothesized to be used on structures so large that they cannot be adequately tested within existing facilities (Allen 2021).

Digital twins will also be involved in pushing the boundaries of what is possible in the field of medicine and human health. Ongoing discussions revolve around the potential application of digital twins to model an individual—a personalized virtual twin of oneself that assimilates all historical data into predicting cancer patterns, for instance—opening up new avenues for personalized health care (Wilcox 2022).

The applications may go beyond health, and venture into intriguing landscapes of a "virtual existence." Virtual twins of individuals living in a "metaverse" or other forms of virtual worlds may make it possible for a life without constraints of the physical realm. Through dynamic holograms or avatars that realistically act and react as one would, the prospects of engaging in activities at different locations worldwide without physically being present may be a possibility (European Commission 2022). Some hypothesize instances of these "proxy" digital twins convening meetings on our behalf, or conversing with people who no longer exist in the real world, such as the deceased or even a past, future version of oneself (NTT n.d.).

With the "twinning" of both "things" and "people" achieved, the ability to simulate life to varying degrees on a virtual plain is a truly unique function of the digital twin technologies. Some may argue that immersive gaming experiences enabled by current virtual reality technologies already achieve this feat. Even within the gaming industry, certain companies are working to develop AI capabilities to equip the non-player characters with smaller-scale neural networks of their own to make the game even more realistic (Marr 2023). Furthermore, this is already happening to an extent in the retail industry. Customers now have the opportunity to be fully immersed in a virtual environment whether it is for virtual car viewings and trials, or perusing items on a virtual retail store. Merchandisers are leveraging this solution to observe and enhance the customer experience, ultimately boosting sales (Penedo 2023). Extending beyond the individual experiences in gaming and consumer interactions in retail, the scale of a virtual "metaverse" may encompass entire enterprises, industries, and cities (Author Year; McKinsey 2022).

As businesses and countries continue to digitalize and adopt digital twins' enabling technologies, the future may see a unification of multiple digital twins. The latest report on the digital twin market revealed that 75% of the firms that use Internet of Things (IoT) stated that they benefit from using digital twins or plan to fully deploy it within a year (Simsek 2023). Given the increasing adoption of IoT and the benefits that it entails from real-time data, the demand for these solutions will continue to grow as businesses look to embrace digital twins for operational performance optimization and quality control management.

The adoption of digital twins have also reportedly helped businesses navigate their digital expansion initiatives. According to the Equinix 2023 Global Tech Trends Survey, most of the IT decision-makers in Asia and the Pacific have already implemented digital twins into their operations to improve business performance (Equinix 2023). Among these respondents, over 80% are already implementing AI in IT and cybersecurity functions. This signifies that in the Asia and the Pacific region, AI and digital twins will be the predominant driving forces behind business expansion.

Lastly, digital twins are increasingly becoming more prominent in addressing climate change. Many organizations are exploring digital twins as a tool to address their greenhouse gas (GHG) emissions, primarily due to their ability to replicate real-world conditions and report real-time information. The potential of digital twin solutions to help bridge the infrastructure gap is further discussed below.

C. Potential to Bridge the Infrastructure Investment Gap and Strengthen Resilience in Asia and the Pacific

The average annual infrastructure investment required in 45 developing economies in Asia and the Pacific from 2016 to 2030 amounts to an estimated $1.7 trillion (Figure A13.4), provided growth conditions are sustained within the region with consistent efforts to respond to climate change. Among these ADB members, the power and transport sectors require the most amount of investment, taking up almost 90% of the annual infrastructure investment needs with only 50% of ADB's commitment in 2019 going into these sectors. An estimate of the infrastructure investment gap—the difference between investment needs and current investment levels—across 25 of these economies found that it amounted to 2.4% of the projected gross domestic product for the period 2016-2020 when considering climate mitigation and adaptation costs (ADB 2017).

Figure A13.4: Annual Infrastructure Investment Needs by Sector in Developing Asia and the Pacific

Unit: $ Billion (Bn), average for 2016-2030

Source: Adapted from ADB data.

Projects related to the infrastructure sector necessitate some of the most significant decision-making and can often be a complex process requiring thorough assessment of risks, which are not always visible in the absence of enabling technologies. Within the infrastructure sector comprising transport, power, water, and communications, the concept of digital twins being implemented is proving to be less of an intrusive innovation and more of a "natural point of convergence."

Digital twins are being deployed to meet sustainability goals. Given that Southeast Asia ranks among the highest in climate risk exposure, digital twins can foreseeably add value to infrastructure projects and emission-intensive sectors by providing visibility, analysis, and insight into the engineering elements of an asset. For example, digital twins can provide descriptive datasets on GHG emissions over a project's lifespan, which facilitates informed decision-making and effectively helps engineers incorporate solutions for GHG emission mitigation.

It is anticipated that in about 3 decades, urbanization levels would rise and approximately 80% of the global population will be living in cities (Venditti 2022). Therefore, the need to make infrastructure adaptable and ensure responsiveness to evolving migration and urbanization trends and demographic shifts is a driving force to narrow the infrastructure investment discrepancy. Investing in digital twins in the infrastructure sector may reap certain value-added benefits. For instance, in the People's Republic of China, a virtual twin of a meteorological radar tower was created ahead of construction. This smart construction provides a transparent approach enhancing design efficiency by almost 30% and reduced the construction process error rate by almost 60% (Dassault Systèmes n.d.). In general, research suggests that governments can achieve approximately $9 return on investment (ROI) for every $1 spent on digital twins for infrastructure, but could yield an ROI of up to $30 for every $1 invested (Gazula n.d.).

Digital twins can maximize infrastructure ROI by minimizing costs and delivering superior results, which can ultimately aid in closing the infrastructure investment gaps in key regions that ADB is supporting. Some other considerations on the role digital twins can play in infrastructure development and construction include the following:

Digital twins ensure safety in infrastructure projects.
Workforce safety is a key priority for infrastructure projects. Digital twins can be used to simulate various scenarios and identify potential safety hazards before the asset is built. Using digital twins as a proactive tool in addressing early-stage workforce safety ensures that construction sites are safe for both workers and future occupants.

Developers can avoid costly mistakes and improve project outcomes.
Engineers can test infrastructure designs using accurate 3D models that are also up-to-date with near-to-real time data from or near the built environment. This feature allows engineers to simulate alternative scenarios before any construction is initiated, allowing them to identify potential issues early on to minimize costs in relation to late-stage adjustments and changes.

Digital twins enable improved project collaboration across key stakeholders.
Digital twins provide an integrated visualization of previously siloed information, allowing stakeholders to interact with the virtual representation of the infrastructure asset. This fosters improved communication, enhancing coordination to ensure all relevant parties are involved and aligned throughout all stages of the project development. Key characteristics of a project can be assessed early in the project, enabling timely modifications throughout the project's life cycle. This also streamlines the decision-making process, which saves time and minimize mistakes.

Digital twins reinforce stakeholder buy-in.
Since digital twins can facilitate realistic virtual replicas of an infrastructure asset, and also provide an immersive virtual experience, stakeholders can gain a more comprehensive understanding of the infrastructure projects they are engaged in. The extensive visualization of engineering elements, and the value-added benefits aid in securing stakeholder buy-in, which helps secure infrastructure investments.

Beyond construction, digital twins also hold significant potential for achieving long-term cost savings in the maintenance of infrastructure projects. One of the main issues facing infrastructure asset owners is the maintenance costs that stem from poor quality designs and substandard construction. Digital twins enable continuous monitoring and observation of infrastructure performance, and through the integration of additional data, can simulate the implications of various factors allowing for predictive maintenance. For instance, the Maharashtra Metro Rail Corporation implemented a digital twin during the design phase of the project with the goal of eliminating information loss, which was estimated to save $222 million over the 25-year operation of the metro rail system (Zeiss 2019). More importantly, digital twins can also prevent the failure of its real-world sibling and save lives. For instance, in April 2021, the digital twin of the Stavå bridge in Norway monitored by the Norwegian Public Roads Administration detected an anomaly, which if not detected may have led to a catastrophic failure of the bridge. In this case, the rapid response prompted by the digital twin was crucial to ensuring public safety. Similarly, with millions of aging bridges around the world, with approximately 7.5% of the bridges in the United States and over 25% of the bridges in Japan being over 50 years old, digital twins could preempt structural failures in such critical infrastructure, both reducing hefty replacement costs and saving lives.

Ultimately, digital twins can help address the infrastructure investment gap by providing governments and asset owners with a platform for collaboration, and a way to improve planning, performance, and resource allocation. Maximizing the available budget and addressing operational requirements while minimizing costs are critical factors that can help close this gap.

BIBLIOGRAPHY

Abi Research. 2021. The Use of Digital Twins for Urban Planning to Yield US$280 Billion in Cost Savings By 2030. https://www.abiresearch.com/press/use-digital-twins-urban-planning-yield-us280-billion-cost-savings-2030/.

AccuCities. n.d. Digital Twin Industry Map by Symmetry Dimensions. https://www.accucities.com/digital-twin-industry-map-by-symmetry-dimensions/.

Akselos. n.d. Exploring the Industrial Metaverse: Digital Twins and Beyond. https://akselos.com/exploring-the-industrial-metaverse-digital-twins/.

Asian Development Bank (ADB). 2014. *Space Technology and Geographic Information Systems Applications in ADB Projects.* https://www.adb.org/sites/default/files/publication/148901/space-technology-and-gis-applications-adb-projects.pdf.

——. 2017. *Meeting Asia's Infrastructure Needs.* https://www.adb.org/sites/default/files/publication/227496/special-report-infrastructure.pdf. doi:http://dx.doi.org/10.22617/FLS168388-2.

——. 2018. *ADB Strategy 2030: Achieving a Prosperous, Inclusive, Resilient, and Sustainable Asia and the Pacific.* https://www.adb.org/sites/default/files/institutional-document/435391/strategy-2030-main-document.pdf. doi:http://dx.doi.org/10.22617/TCS189401-2.

——. 2019. *Climate Change and Disasters in Asia and the Pacific.* https://events.development.asia/system/files/materials/2019/12/201912-climate-change-and-disasters-asia-and-pacific_1.pdf.

——. 2021. *Digital Technologies for Climate Action, Disaster Resilience, and Environmental Sustainability.* doi:10.22617/TCS210188-2.

——. 2023a. ADB, Indonesia Launch Net Zero Strategy for New Capital. 3 December.

——. 2023b. *Building Greener, Resilient Transport Infrastructure: Innovating with Artificial Intelligence and Digital Twins in Road Design in Uzbekistan.* doi:10.22617/TIM230342.

——. 2023c. ADB's Work in the Urban Development Sector. https://www.adb.org/what-we-do/topics/urban-development/overview.

——. 2023d. ADB's Vision of a Water-Secure and Resilient Asia and Pacific.

——. 2023e. Transport. https://www.adb.org/what-we-do/topics/transport.

——. 2023f. Energy. https://www.adb.org/what-we-do/topics/energy.

Agrawal, A., V. Singh, and M. Fischer. 2022. *A New Perspective on Digital Twins: Imparting Intelligence and Agency to Entities.* IEEE.

Akbar, F. 2024. Transform Your Business with the Capabilities of Digital Twin and AI. *Toobler.* 10 October. https://www.toobler.com/blog/digital-twin-and-ai.

Allahaim, F.S.A. and L. Liu. n.d. An Empirical Classification of Cost Overrun in Infrastructure Projects by Using Cluster Analysis. Fourth International Utzon Symposium–Sydney, Australia. *University of New South Wales.*

Allahaim, F. S. A. and L. Liu. n.d. *An Empirical Classification of Cost Overrun in Infrastructure Projects by Using Cluster Analysis*. University of New South Wales. An Empirical Classification of Cost Overrun in Infrastructure Projects by Using Cluster Analysis.

Altair. n.d. *2022 Digital Twin Survey Report*. https://altair.com/docs/default-source/pdfs/altair_dt-global-survey-report_web.pdf?sfvrsn=457856ab_9.

____. 2023. *Global Digital Twin Survey Report Vertical Breakdown: Banking, Financial Services, and Insurance*. https://altair.com/docs/default-source/resource-library/altair_survey-report_bsfi.pdf?sfvrsn=6fa8a1c7_1.

Allen, B. D. 2021. Digital Twins and Living Models at NASA. *National Aeronautics and Space Administration*. https://ntrs.nasa.gov/citations/20210023699.

Amazon Web Services (AWS). n.d. What is Digital Twin Technology? https://aws.amazon.com/what-is/digital-twin/.

American Architects. 2017. The Macleamy Curve. In S. Talebi. 2014. *Exploring Advantages and Challenges of Adaptation and Implementation of BIM in Project Life Cycle*. Paper for the 2nd BIM International Conference on Challenges to Come.

Andrade, A. 2022. The 4 Levels of the Digital Twin Technology–2024. *Vidya*. https://vidyatec.com/blog/the-4-levels-of-the-digital-twin-technology/.

Armstrong, M.M. n.d. *Cheat Sheet: What is Digital Twin?* IBM.

Bentley. n.d. Digital Twins in the Process Industry. Executive Brief. https://www.bentley.com/wp-content/uploads/eBook-Executive-Brief-Digital-Twins-Process-Industry-EN.pdf.

Bhoda, S. K. 2024. The Role of AI and Machine Learning in Enhancing Digital Twins. *LinkedIn*. https://www.linkedin.com/pulse/role-ai-machine-learning-enhancing-digital-twins-santosh-kumar-bhoda-uyqec. 24 April.

Big Data Value. 2022. Digital Twins and Standards. *European Big Data Value Forum*. https://european-big-data-value-forum.eu/wp-content/uploads/2022/10/Digital-Twins-and-Standards-v-1-0.pdf.

Blouin, L. 2023. *AI's Mysterious 'Black Box' Problem, Explained*. University of Michigan-Dearborn. https://umdearborn.edu/news/ais-mysterious-black-box-problem-explained. 6 March.

Bui, T. X. 2023. 56th Hawaii International Conference on System Sciences (HICCS). Hyatt Regency Maui, 3–6 January. University of Hawaii at Manoa.

Bündnis Entwicklung Hilft. 2022. World Risk Report. https://weltrisikobericht.de/wp-content/uploads/2022/09/WorldRiskReport-2022_Online.pdf.

Celtic Anglian Water (CAW). 2024. BIM in Water Infrastructure: A Tool for Progress. https://www.caw.ie/2024/02/bim-in-water-infrastructure-a-tool-for-progress/.

Cisco. n.d. How Do OT and IT Differ? https://www.cisco.com/c/en/us/solutions/internet-of-things/what-is-ot-vs-it.html#~uniting-it-and-ot-teams.

Cisco Digital Readiness Index. 2021. https://www.cisco.com/c/en/us/about/csr/research-resources/digital-readiness.html.

Cosmas, A. et al. 2024. Digital Twins and Generative AI: A Powerful Pairing. https://www.mckinsey.com/capabilities/mckinsey-digital/our-insights/tech-forward/digital-twins-and-generative-ai-a-powerful-pairing.

Dassault Systèmes. n.d. CSADI: Using Industry Solutions. https://www.3ds.com/insights/customer-stories/csadi-smart-construction.

Dassault Systèmes and Accenture. 2021. *The Critical Role of Virtual Twins in Accelerating Sustainability*. https://www.3ds.com/assets/invest/2021-01/dassault-systemes-and-accenture-virtual-twin-and-sustainability.pdf.

Data Bridge. 2023. Asia-Pacific Digital Twin Financial Services and Insurance Market—Industry Trends and Forecast to 2030. https://www.databridgemarketresearch.com/reports/asia-pacific-digital-twin-financial-services-and-insurance-market.

Eckstein, D., M.-L Hutfils, and M. Winges. 2018. *Global Climate Risk Index 2019*. https://www.germanwatch.org/en/16046.

Equinix. 2023. Global Tech Trends Survey: The Benefits and Challenges of New Digital Technologies, and Future-Proofing Strategies. https://www.equinix.com/resources/infopapers/equinix-tech-trends-survey.

European Big Data Value Association. 2022. Digital Twins and Standards. *European Big Data Value Forum.* https://european-big-data-value-forum.eu/wp-content/uploads/2022/10/Digital-Twins-and-Standards-v-1-0.pdf.
Field, H. and L. Feiner. 2023. *Biden Issues U.S.' First AI Executive Order, Requiring Safety Assessments, Civil Rights Guidance, Research on Labor Market Impact. CNBC.*

European Commission. 2022. Meet Your Digital Twin, A Virtual Version of Yourself. https://cordis.europa.eu/article/id/441913-trending-science-meet-your-digital-twin-a-virtual-version-of-yourself.

Fenstermaker. 2022. What is a Digital Twin? https://blog.fenstermaker.com/what-is-a-digital-twin/.

Fenwick, Elliott. n.d. The Challenges and Legal Implications of Digital Twins. https://www.fenwickelliott.com/research-insight/annual-review/2020/challenges-legal-implications-digital-twins.

Fortune Business Insights. n.d. Asia Pacific Digital Twin Market Size, Share & COVID-19 Impact Analysis, By Type (Parts Twin, Product Twin, Process Twin, and System Twin), By Application (Predictive Maintenance, Business Optimization, Product Design & Development, and Others), By End-user (Aerospace & Defense, Automotive & Transportation, Manufacturing, Healthcare, Retail, Energy & Utilities, Home & Commercial, IT and Telecom, and Others), and Regional Forecast, 2023–2030. https://www.fortunebusinessinsights.com/asia-pacific-digital-twin-market-107451.

Gartner. 2023. Gartner Says Cloud Will Become a Business Necessity by 2028. Press release. 29 November. https://www.gartner.com/en/newsroom/press-releases/2023-11-29-gartner-says-cloud-will-become-a-business-necessity-by-2028#:~:text=The%20Role%20of%20Cloud%20in%202023&text=In%202023%2C%20organizations%20are%20using,to%20accelerate%20their%20business%20initiatives. 29 November.

———. n.d. Definition of Digital Twin - IT Glossary. Gartner.

Gazula, N. and C. Earp. 2023. Digital Twins: Catalyst for Transformative Infrastructure. *KPMG*. https://kpmg.com/ca/en/home/insights/2024/03/digital-twins.html.

GE Digital. 2016. *Minds + Machines: Meet A Digital Twin.* A video.

Georgia Institute of Technology. 2019. Smart City Digital Twin Convergence Workshop: FINAL REPORT. https://smartcitydigitaltwins.gatech.edu/sites/default/files/documents/scdt/smart_city_digital_twin_convergence_workshop_final_report.pdf.

Google Cloud. n.d. Generate Text, Images, Code, and More with Google Cloud AI. https://cloud.google.com/use-cases/generative-ai.

Grieves, M. W. 2020. Digital Twin: Developing a 21st Century Product Model. In P. A. Cola, K. J. Lyytinen, and S.A. Nartker, eds. Voices of Practitioner Scholars in Management. Orange Frazer Press.

____. 2023. *Digital Twins and IoT Integrating the Physical and Virtual Worlds.* Nextspace.

Grieves, M. and J. Vickers. 2017. Digital Twin: Mitigating Unpredictable, Undesirable Emergent Behavior in Complex Systems. . In: Kahlen, J., Flumerfelt, S., Alves, A. (eds) Transdisciplinary Perspectives on Complex Systems. Springer.

Grunitz, M. 2023. Digital Twins—A Beginner's Guide. *WeAreBrain.* 10 April. https://wearebrain.com/blog/digital-twins-beginners-guide/.

Harkat, G. D. and K. Kasat. 2019. Introductory Chapter: Artificial Intelligence—Challenges and Applications. In *Artificial Intelligence—Scope and Limitations*. IntechOpen. doi:10.5772/intechopen.84624.

Helbing, D. and J.A. Sánchez-Vaquerizo. 2022. *Digital Twins: Potentials, Ethical Issues, and Limitations*. Handbook on the Politics and Governance of Big Data and Artificial Intelligence.

IBM. n. d. What is Edge Computing? https://www.ibm.com/topics/edge-computing.

International Foundation for Valuing Impacts, Inc. and Value Balancing Alliance. 2024. Greenhouse Gas Emissions: Topic Methodology (Exposure Draft). IFVI_VBA_Public Exposure DRAFT_GHG_Methodology_A4.pdf.

Jovanovic, B. and P.L. Rousseau. 2005. *General Purpose Technologies*. http://www.nber.org/papers/w11093.

Kapteyn, M. G., D.J. Knezevic, and K.E. Willcox. *Toward Predictive Digital Twins via Component-Based Reduced-Order Models and Interpretable Machine Learning*. American Institute of Aeronautics and Astronautics, Inc.

Kim, Y.-W., S. Yoo, H. Lee, and S. Han. 2023. *Survey of Digital Twin Maturity Models.* https://www.researchgate.net/profile/Yong-Woon-Kim-4/publication/346470132_Digital_Twin_maturity_model/links/6226bde09f7b32463417a1f2/Digital-Twin-maturity-model.pdf.

Kreuzer, T., P. Papapetrou, and J. Zdravkovic. 2024. Artificial Intelligence in Digital Twins—A Systematic Literature Review. *Data Knowl Eng.* 151: 102304.

Kritzinger, W., M. Karner, G. Traar, J. Henjes, and W. Sihn. 2018. Digital Twin in Manufacturing: A Categorical Literature Review and Classification. *IFAC-PapersOnLine.* 51: 1016–1022.

Lal, A., J. Dang, C. Nabzdyk, O. Gajic, and V. Herasevich. 2022. Regulatory Oversight and Ethical Concerns Surrounding Software as Medical Device (SaMD) and Digital Twin Technology in Healthcare. *Ann Transl Med.* 10(18)950.

Liu, Z. et al. 2023. Digital Twin for Predictive Maintenance. In *NDE 4.0, Predictive Maintenance, Communication, and Energy Systems: The Digital Transformation of NDE.* Conference paper. doi:10.1117/12.2660270.

Luxton, D. D. 2016. An Introduction to Artificial Intelligence in Behavioral and Mental Health Care. In *Artificial Intelligence in Behavioral and Mental Health Care.* 1–26. Elsevier. doi:10.1016/B978-0-12-420248-1.00001-5.

Mangels, B. 2022. Mirroring Reality: Dr. Michael Grieves on the Past, Present, and Future of Digital Twin. *Physna.* 24 February.

Marr, B. 2016. What Is The Difference Between Artificial Intelligence and Machine Learning? *Forbes.*

_____. 2023. Digital Twins, Generative AI, and the Metaverse. *Forbes.*

McKinsey. 2022. *Digital Twins: The Foundation of the Enterprise Metaverse.* https://www.mckinsey.com/capabilities/mckinsey-digital/our-insights/digital-twins-the-foundation-of-the-enterprise-metaverse.

_____. 2023.*The State of AI in 2023: Generative AI's Breakout Year.* https://www.mckinsey.com/capabilities/quantumblack/our-insights/the-state-of-ai-in-2023-generative-ais-breakout-year#/.

Microsoft Azure. n.d. What is Cloud Computing? https://azure.microsoft.com/en-us/resources/cloud-computing-dictionary/what-is-cloud-computing#:~:text=Simply%20put%2C%20cloud%20computing%20is,resources%2C%20and%20economies%20of%20scale.

_____. 2024. Deep Learning vs. Machine Learning in Azure Machine Learning. https://learn.microsoft.com/en-us/azure/machine-learning/concept-deep-learning-vs-machine-learning?view=azureml-api-2.

MRINETWORK. 2023. Digital Twin Recruitment, and the Challenges HR Managers Face When Hiring Professionals. https://mrinetwork.com/hiring-talent-strategy/digital-twin-recruitment-and-the-challenges-hr-managers-face-when-hiring-professionals/.

NTT. n.d. Human Digital Twins: Creating New Value Beyond the Constraints of the Real World. https://www.rd.ntt/e/ai/0004.html.

Olcott, S. and C. Mullen. 2020. *Digital Twin Consortium Defines Digital Twin.* Digital Twin Consortium.

Panaro, P., S. Parlow, and F. Amman. 2024. How Pairing Digital Twin Technology with AI Could Boost Buildings' Emissions Reductions. https://www.weforum.org/agenda/2024/03/how-digital-twin-technology-can-work-with-ai-to-boost-buildings-emissions-reductions/.

Penedo, L. 2023. Stepping Into the Future of Retail: How Digital Twins Are Transforming the Retail Landscape. https://www.linkedin.com/pulse/stepping-future-retail-how-digital-twins/.

Philp, D. 2021. Blog: Digital Twins and How the Hub's New Interactive Guidance Can Help. Centre for Digital Built Britain.

Pratt, M. K. 2023. *Evil Digital Twins and Other Risks: The Use of Twins Opens Up a Host of New Security Concerns.* CSO. https://www.csoonline.com/article/575253/evil-digital-twins-and-other-risks-the-use-of-twins-opens-up-a-host-of-new-security-concerns.html.

Raghunathan, V. 2019. The Path to Digital Twins. *Entrepreneur.* 16 April. https://www.entrepreneur.com/en-au/technology/the-path-to-digital-twins/332316.

Rasheed, A. 2022. *Digital Twins on AWS: Unlocking Business Value and Outcomes.* Amazon Web Services.

Sharma, A., E. Kosasih, J. Zhang, A. Brintrup, and A. Calinescu. 2022. Digital Twins: State of the Art Theory and Practice, Challenges, and Open Research Questions. *J Ind Inf Integr.* 30. 100383.

H . Şimşek. 2023. Discover Top 8 Digital Twin Trends in 2023. AIMultiple. https://research.aimultiple.com/digital-twin-trends/#further-reading.

Synengco. n.d. Digital Twin: The Future is Here. https://synengco.com/digital-twin-the-future-is-here/.

Strauss, P. 2023. Revolutionising 'Intelligent Environments': How Generative AI and Digital Twins are Changing YOUR Game. https://www.linkedin.com/pulse/revolutionising-intelligent-environments-how-ai-twins-strauss-msc/.

The Insight Partners. 2022. Cloud Computing Market Outlook, Trend, Share Analysis till 2028. https://www.theinsightpartners.com/reports/cloud-computing-market.

TNO. 2022. *TNO Report: A Detailed Study of Digital Twins for Wind Energy Applications.* https://publications.tno.nl/publication/34641535/ug1XOG/TNO-2022-R12367.pdf.

Trajtenberg, M. 2018. *AI as the Next GPT: A Political-Economy Perspective.* National Bureau of Economic Research. https://www.nber.org/system/files/working_papers/w24245/w24245.pdf.

TWI. n.d. What is a Digital Twin Technology and How Does it Work? https://www.twi-global.com/technical-knowledge/faqs/what-is-digital-twin.

txOne Networks. 2023. *Digital Twins: The Benefits and Challenges of Revolutionary Technology in Automotive Industries*. https://www.txone.com/blog/digital-twins-benefits-and-challenges-revolutionary-technology-in-automotive-industries/.

Venditti, B. 2022. This Chart Shows the Impact Rising Urbanization Will Have on the World. *World Economic Forum.* 26 April.

Willcox, K. 2022. How 'Digital Twins' Could Help Us Predict the Future. TED. https://www.ted.com/talks/karen_willcox_how_digital_twins_could_help_us_predict_the_future.

World Economic Forum. 2022. Digital Twin Cities: Framework and Global Practices. https://www3.weforum.org/docs/WEF_Global_Digital_Twin_Cities_Framework_and_Practice_2022.pdf.

Zeiss, G. 2019. 3D BIM + Geospatial Full Life Cycle Metro Rail Project Aims at Eliminating Data Loss. https://www.geospatialworld.net/blogs/3d-bim-geospatial-full-lifecycle-metro-rail-project/.

Zhang, M. et al. 2022. Digital Twin Data: Methods and Key Technologies. *Digital Twin.* 1, 2.

www.ingramcontent.com/pod-product-compliance
Lightning Source LLC
Chambersburg PA
CBHW041756220926
51847CB00014B/223
* 9 7 8 9 2 9 2 7 7 2 9 6 3 *